GET MARRIED for CHRIST'S SAKE

KENNY JACKSON

CREATION
HOUSE

GET MARRIED FOR CHRIST'S SAKE by Kenny Jackson
Published by Creation House Books
A Charisma Media Company
600 Rinehart Road
Lake Mary, Florida 32746
www.charismamedia.com

Unless otherwise noted, all Scripture quotations are from the Holy Bible, New International Version. Copyright © 1973, 1978, 1984, International Bible Society. Used by permission

Scripture quotations marked KJV are from the King James Version of the Bible.

Scripture quotations marked NKJV are from the New King James Version of the Bible. Copyright © 1979, 1980, 1982 by Thomas Nelson, Inc., publishers. Used by permission.

Scripture quotations marked NAS are from the New American Standard Bible—Updated Edition, Copyright © 1960, 1962, 1963, 1968, 1971, 1972, 1973, 1975, 1977, 1995 by The Lockman Foundation. Used by permission. (www.Lockman.org)

Design Director: Bill Johnson
Cover design by Rachel Lopez
Author portrait by Hailey Bland

Visit the author's website: www.KingdomSexuality.com

Library of Congress Cataloging-in-Publication Data: 2011925312
International Standard Book Number: 978-1-61638-501-9

First edition

11 12 13 14 15 A 9 8 7 6 5 4 3 2 1
Printed in Canada

Dedication

I'm dedicating a portion of this book to people not yet born—my children's children. Hopefully by the time you're old enough to care, I will have succeeded in bribing your parents into making this book required reading before you reach middle school.

I also dedicate this book to the memory of the woman who made me think I could do and be anything I could ever imagine— my mom, Dorothy Marie Jackson, whose marriage to my awesome, godly Dad, William Harrison Jackson, lasted forty-four years until she passed. I miss her too, Pop.

Finally, to my very breath—Maria. We did it, Babe! And now, for our little inside joke…You'd better be careful!!!

Acknowledgments

A LONG LIST OF people had some level of influence on getting this book to print. Sandi Tompkins deserves a huge "Thank You" for sending me that e-mail invitation to meet Patti Hummel. Ray and Emily Duenke, and Bill and Nancy Brown can write the book on fruitful parenting. I love you guys. I still owe Patricia Vera and Diane Chandler ice cream and coffee, respectively, for proofreading my first draft a long time ago. Alissa and Kenny Carpenter, Bryan and Tara Riley, James and Kelli Bishop, and my youngest son, Micah, all put their money where their hearts were. They know what I mean. I also want to thank Elaine Wright Colvin for making me feel, in a college writing class, like I might actually have something to say.

Finally, I want to thank the Author and Finisher of my faith. I love you, Abba Father!

Table of Contents

Foreword

G OD CREATED MARRIAGE when He formed from Adam's DNA the woman named Eve. They were both created in the image of God; and from this loving union came the family. Men and women are equal: different in gender, but equal in the eyes of God. Therefore they must be equal in the eyes of each of us. Men and women are equal in value, equal in calling, equal in purpose—but also different, according to each one's unique gifts and callings. It's the differences between ministry partners that bring the most synergy. The diversity passed on generation after generation simply multiplies the impact.

The influence inherent in the family is the greatest influence in the world. I often counsel young couples and I speak on this topic while discussing marriage: that love is really a triangle. God is at the top of a triangle, each one of them are on either side of the triangle's base. The foundation is in truth and love. The more they function from that foundation of truth and love, the closer they move to God and the closer they become to each other. It's from that triangle of love that they can impact an entire world.

Kenny Jackson was only a teenager when I was speaking at a youth gathering of fifteen thousand young people called "Fish Net" in Virginia. Darlene, my wife, was with me. She was counseling the youth and got to meet Kenny for the first time. I've admired Kenny, his musical skills in playing the saxophone and singing. His performances were used to multiply the message of the gospel as he traveled with the YWAM team called Far

East Evangelism Team out of Hong Kong (better known as the F.E.E.T team). There a handsome African American met a Korean young lady named Maria, fell in love, and got married— from two cultures and ethnicities came a union that was powerful for God. From that diversity in a spirit of unity God has used them to touch multitudes. I know their three beautiful children. I've watched them grow up as missionary kids: David, Mia and Micah. As teenagers presently, they hardly realize the great potential and strengths that are within them, but already they influence others. We are thankful for this family and what they mean to the kingdom of God.

Kenny is writing out of his life that is a life surrounded by love, dedicated to Christ, and his work that is bringing people into the kingdom of God through Jesus Christ. He shares from the richness of their work in many nations and continents, the blessing, the role, the joy, the challenge of family life in the mission. If it works in missionary life, it will work anywhere. I commend Kenny Jackson and his book *Get Married for Christ's Sake*. It will bless you.

—Loren Cunningham
Founder of Youth With A Mission

Preface

RUCKLOADS OF BOOKS exist on the topic of marriage. Most people only read those books after they are so far along in a relationship that it is almost impossible to change course, even if they are heading for disaster!

Although *Get Married for Christ's Sake* is designed to especially benefit Christian singles seriously considering marriage, you stand to benefit from this book—regardless of your marital status—by taking a fresh look at a bigger picture of marriage than you may have considered before.

Many marriages crash and burn because people were not careful about whom they became emotionally involved with in the first place. God is the best one to guide us through the maze.

This book's inception began when one of our dear friends called off his wedding only a few days before the big day. As my wife and I spent time coaching the couple through the fallout, it became clear that had they both been familiar with some of the principles in this book, *before* getting emotionally attached, much of the pain and regret they and their family members endured could have been avoided. There is a big difference between planning a wedding and preparing for marriage.

Social science research often confirms that people who commit violent crimes tend to be the offspring of deficient parenting and broken homes.

Books are read one page at a time, in sequential order. Most of the time, however, marriage doesn't work that way! Marital challenges come our way from various directions, often, all at the same time, and in random order!

The first few chapters of *Get Married for Christ's Sake* are intended to be a wake-up call to readers who think that the euphoria they feel (typically called "love") is sufficient to ensure a happy, successful marriage that lasts forever. These chapters are an attempt to paint the big picture of what happens socially and spiritually when a man and woman join their lives. You will be challenged to consider some of the glorious, but often overlooked, possibilities of a marriage that has been prepared for thoughtfully and prayerfully.

The institution of marriage suffers fierce opposition these days. State governments increasingly endorse same-sex marriage, which has snowballed into a movement that promises to drastically change the landscape of marriage and the family as we have known it. Hollywood movies, supposedly reflecting real life back to us, have normalized the idea of "shacking up." There is little or no sense of obligation to formalize intimate relationships anymore.

Hebrews 13:14 says, "Marriage should be honored by all." My wife, Maria, and I hope *Get Married for Christ's Sake* will increase your respect for, and awe of, marriage as God's glorious design and the critical building block of every social structure.

—KENNY JACKSON

Introduction

so sad - wow!

NEARLY 50 PERCENT of Christian marriages end in divorce. How does that make you feel? Most of us simply shake our heads and say, "Wow. That's pretty sad." However, we cannot seem to think of much else to do.

What if 50 percent of all skydives ended in death? What if 50 percent of all airplanes crashed? What if 50 percent of all meals served at fast-food restaurants were poison? How would we react if these situations were reality? People would gladly sacrifice sleep, food, and even payment to work on finding solutions. There would be the kind of urgent response and solidarity that was witnessed on September 11, 2001. In a matter of minutes, four hijacked airplanes crashed on US soil. On that terrible day there were more than two thousand airplanes in the air at the time. Four is a relatively low percentage. But because human lives were at risk, people worldwide were moved to act.

What action are you taking to do something about the 50 percent divorce rate among God's people? Is this not an emergency worth dropping everything for in order to find a solution? *Amen!*.

Jesus prayed, "Father, make them one." We read that prayer as if He was only praying for His disciples. What would the world's response to the gospel be if the message were being presented by a church that really looks like God's kingdom on the earth, which includes solid marriages that have what it takes to go the distance?

How many of us consider marriage preparation as essential

as the preparation required for safe skydiving? Many couples take the leap into matrimony as if the only preparation required are the rings, dress, cake, a preacher, flowers, and the invitations. Those are definitely important factors when it comes to preparing for the wedding day. Is it not also necessary to prepare for the *years* that follow "the big day"?

In America, the average parent spends twelve to thirteen years preparing their kids for college. Parents can face legal prosecution for not providing their children appropriate education during their developing years. College lasts at least four years, and for some people, seven. Marriage is meant to last a lifetime! Yet few Christians spend more than a day or two in premarital counseling with their pastor. How much effort and time should go into preparing for this marathon called marriage? What are some of the most important things to consider before jumping out of the airplane of singleness? Let's find out!

1

Why Marriage?

IS MARRIAGE SOLELY for our own enjoyment, benefit, and pleasure? Or could it be that marriage is a crucial component in God's strategy for reaching the lost with the good news of Jesus?

Who "owns" the institution of marriage? Are our marriages really "ours" to do whatever we want with: to save, maintain, improve, throw away, and abandon? Or does God possibly have any say in how our marriages end up? What if He *does* have the majority stake in all marriages, especially Christian ones? Like any other property owned by someone else, if I'm entrusted with the responsibility to care for that property, then it matters what I choose to do or not to do with it when it is in my care.

In the sixties, the notion of "free love" introduced a major shift into Western culture. It became popular and acceptable to enjoy the benefits of living together (fornication) without the legally and morally-binding commitment of marriage.

Jesus lived a relatively short time on the earth, so He did not have time to waste His words. Therefore, whatever He said must have been important. Consequently, for Jesus to take time to actually reference Genesis 2:24 and elaborate on the concept of marriage, it must have been important:

So exciting to think about.

> For this reason a man will leave his father and mother and be united to his wife, and the two will become one flesh. So they are no longer two, but one. Therefore what God has joined together, let man not separate.
>
> —Matthew 19:5–7

That last part is the bit I want to touch on for a moment: "Therefore what God has joined together..." Unfortunately, we have allowed the real heart and meaning of this passage of Scripture to drift into some cute little verse that we "stick in there" at Christian weddings. Our attitude and handling of this enormously insightful Scripture reminds me of a trick I used to attempt to play on my parents when I was a kid. You've probably done it, too.

I would unwrap a stick of chewing gum- stuff the gum in my mouth, and then refold the aluminum wrapper the same way it was when gum was inside. Then I would slip the aluminum wrapper back into the outer paper wrapping. It ended up looking like a normal stick of chewing gum. Finally it was time to offer some unsuspecting victim (usually my parents) a stick of chewing gum, amused by my secret fact that they were only holding an illusion of reality.

What I was offering them was the *appearance* of something of value, but in actual fact, there was *no value* inside whatsoever. My "excited" victim (adults would usually play along) would be duped (as far as I knew) into thinking that their mouth-watering satisfaction was just moments away.

Sometimes we treat Scripture the same way. It becomes the wrapping paper on something we want to *appear* as if it has kingdom value.

I've made several trips to Japan in my lifetime. In recent years there has been a major trend toward "full-service," "Western-style weddings." This involves the bridal gown, veil, flowers, tux, a chapel with pews, an altar, and, if you can afford one, an actual "foreign" guy (American) to conduct the service. The odd thing about these wedding chapels is, they mean nothing more than an element in the total wedding "package." Most of the people getting married in the so-called "chapels" have no Christian faith whatsoever. And no wedding chapel would be complete without a cross, a couple of Bibles and hymnals strategically placed, and maybe even a pipe organ for the deluxe package!

Religious symbolism, which had formerly served as an outward expression of real, life-altering faith has been reduced to a façade, devoid of the slightest understanding of the meaning behind these symbols.

Back to our Scripture. Jesus says, "What God has joined together..." Without getting into the whole debate about predestination vs. random chance, consider the possibility that there may be more involved in coming together with your spouse than just attraction to one another. What might be the implications of the idea that God has taken some initiative in the "joining together"? What if our oneness might have some purpose that goes beyond our compelling love for each other?

An interesting thing to note is that in the first part of this passage from the Book of Matthew, Jesus is quoting the original text found in Genesis 2:24. The last part of the verse is in His own words. The "what God has joined together" bit is Jesus's own implicational conclusion, challenging the hearers (or readers) to consider that their marriage may not only be about them.

GOD'S ORIGINAL DESIGN

To be able to truly see a clearer picture of God's original design for society and how marriage is the foundation for it, we need to look at the two major "beginnings" of human civilization, (i.e., Adam and Eve, and Noah).

Let's go all the way back to the very first man to get an understanding of where God was going in this whole area. There's hardly anyplace better to gain insight than what is available in Genesis 2:18. The Lord says it's not good for the man to be alone. God says He will make a "helper suitable for [Adam]." It is at this point that we see the efficiency of God. God never wastes His efforts. In one act of creation, God:

1. Makes a helper for Adam.

2. Makes the helper attractive to Adam, and it is implied that she finds him attractive as well.

3. Establishes the possibility for reproduction of the "kind."

If physical assistance was all the Lord was after, it would seem logical that God would simply have created another man to help Adam with the workload in the garden. No! God was accomplishing many things at the same time not the least of which would be human reproduction.

If I were God, I would simply have taken some more dust from the earth, formed this suitable helper, and breathed life into the helper, just like with Adam. Instead, the Lord puts Adam into a deep sleep. Then God opens his side, removes a rib, and forms Eve out of that rib. He also makes her a living soul. Genesis 2:24–25 states:

> That is why a man will leave his father and mother and is united to his *wife*, and they will become one flesh. Adam and his *wife* were both naked, and they felt no shame.
> Not girlfriend but wife!   —Emphasis added

So, one of the first things God did was make two naked people whose physical intimacy would involve no sense of shame (not even with God around!). They were made for each other—literally—and formed the very first marriage.

This Scripture also demonstrates that Adam was not going to require more than one of these "suitable" helpers. In other words, not only was it a heterosexual relationship, it was also monogamous.

Reading further along in the Genesis account, it doesn't take long to see the implications of Adam and Eve's open door to sin and its impact on human society. Wickedness and evil had so permeated humanity that God was sorry He had even made man in the first place. (Gens 6:6).

So, what does God do? He starts all over. However, He does not choose to wipe out the entire "batch." God's creation and original design was such good quality, even though they misused their free will in such a way that God would have to destroy the majority before the majority destroyed the whole, that He was able to find eight people worth saving. But these eight were not simply eight random, unrelated individuals. God restarted the human race with *four marriages!* Noah, his wife, and Noah's three sons and their wives would be the foundation for human society on the earth once the water subsided. Four marriages. One family.

The reason I have taken the time to remind us of this very basic historical perspective is because the society we are becoming is rapidly losing respect of the idea that *marriage is the superglue that holds everything in our society together.* The day that notion becomes too old fashioned or bothersome to maintain, that will be the day that marks the end of human civilization as we have known it.

When I started working on this book a few years ago, My initial title was going to be *Marriage Prep*. Unfortunately, the longer I took writing the book, the more drastically society was imploding all around me. The so-called "gay rights" movement,

I pray that doesn't happen.

for example, has escalated to the place where (as of this writing) seven countries have officially legalized same-sex unions, calling them "marriage":

1. The Netherlands, April 1, 2001

2. Belgium, January 30, 2003

3. Spain, June 30, 2005

4. Canada, July 20, 2005

5. South Africa, November 30, 2006

6. Norway, January 1, 2009

7. Sweden, May 1, 2009[1]

The United States of America is in turmoil over whether or not the definition of marriage can continue meaning what it has always meant from the beginning of humanity. As of this writing, nine American states are in some stage of recognizing same-sex "marriage." They include Massachusetts, Connecticut, Vermont, Maine, Iowa, New Hampshire, New York, Washington, DC, and California. Approximately eleven thousand same-sex couples were married in California within the first three months of legalization in that state alone![2]

Biblical marriage is truly in trouble, yet homosexuality is not its only threat. Postmodern Christians are being gradually sedated into the exact same casual attitude toward marriage as the rest of the world. Christian marriages are ending in divorce at the same rate as everybody else. So, what value is marriage anyway?

Now that the definition of marriage has evolved into including the non-biblical practice of same-gender unions, I will be using the term *biblical marriage* to mean a publicly recognized covenant between one man, one woman, and God. Does that sound familiar?

Most American Christians between the ages of seventeen and thirty, if asked for a definition of the word "family," would feel awkward defining it as a father, mother, and children living together.

Worldwide, societies commemorate everything but *marriage* (birthdays, national holidays, memorial days, etc.). We pay athletes millions of dollars to show us what they can do with a ball, yet society's view of an elderly couple celebrating sixty years of marriage, for example, is, "Aw, aren't they cute!"

It's more than cute! It is often an achievement worthy of the highest medal of honor we can come up with. Such an accomplishment represents years of sacrifices, promises kept, forgiveness asked for, apologies accepted, laughs and tears, joy and shared dreams, gains and losses.

I pray I cannot be blessed with that

Biblical marriage (not independent, "self-made" individuals) is the *core* component of human civilization. When the balance of what is considered normal shifts from biblical marriage to something other than that, humanity's self-destruction is certain to follow.

heartbreaking

Sadly, we spend more time preparing for the wedding day than we do for marriage. Biblical marriage is supposed to be one of the most important decisions we make in our lives. It is supposed to last until "death us do part." What's the problem?

Part of the problem is that Christian young women mainly see marriage as the sole solution to their need to feel loved, while Christian young men see it primarily as the opportunity to finally and "lawfully" release all of their pent-up sexual tension. There is nothing inherently wrong with either of those motivations. However, lots more preparation is required for the other 80 percent of what a lifelong marriage is all about!

guilty of that at times

9

THE ROAD TO MARRIAGE

I was recently addressing a small class of middle school kids on the topic of boy/girl relationships. My first question to the class was, "How many of you think you will get married someday?" Slightly caught off guard, several sheepishly raised their hands with a confused look on their faces.

The next question was, "How many know that you definitely *want* to get married someday?" True to my expectations, most of the girls had no problem raising their hands right away for that one. A smaller percentage of the boys responded with any relative degree of certainty.

The follow-up question set the tone for the rest of our lessons together:

"How many of you are on the road to marriage?" No hands, but lots of furled brows and very confused faces. Allowing the question to digest for a good while, I launched into my thesis statement for the week:

"Congratulations! Whether you realize it or not, you are 'on the road to marriage' right now!" I remember the shocked look on one blond little boy's face. I immediately asked him how he felt about that fact. He said, "Scared." Perfect! That's just the response I was hoping for. What his adorable response really indicated was a healthy *respect* for everything that marriage is supposedly all about.

This book is designed for Christian singles who have never been married before. It's not a marriage repair kit for people who have made all the mistakes makeable. Nor is it for divorced singles who are hoping to get it right the next time around. This book has a twofold mission:

1. To highlight God's ultimate, original purpose for marriage in society.

2. To guide Christian singles (who have never been married before) into how to safeguard, preserve, and prepare themselves while on the road toward that potentially world-changing status in life.

So, when do you merge onto the road to marriage? One of the kids said, "When you get engaged." Another shouted, "On your wedding day!" I love enthusiastic students. Eventually, one of the more thoughtful students ventured, "When you're born?" We have a winner! I came up with some kind of cheesy award for the correct answer, and our lesson was underway.

To offer a non-religious answer to the question, "Why marriage?" Rutgers University, as part of a nationwide program called *The Marriage Project*, recently published its findings after studying hundreds of family units around the world. A few of the very basic discoveries they made include:

1. Children raised in a two-parent household with a father and a mother are statistically better off than children raised either in a single-parent household or with unmarried biological parents.

2. The latter tend to:
   a. live in poverty,
   b. be more likely to break the law, and
   c. end up in broken relationships and divorced themselves.[3]

Even without a concept that God is the originator of the idea of marriage and with no understanding of the Bible or its principles of marriage, everyone stands to benefit when marriage is affirmed, encouraged, and perpetuated in any society.

Establishing a Legacy Mind-set

A T A BUSINESS meeting I attended recently, a man introduced himself while handing me his card. He said, "I work for the company that Benjamin Franklin started." Having started one or two failed ventures myself, I was immediately struck by two things. The first being that, although Ben Franklin has been dead for a couple hundred years, a residual expression of a business he started years ago still thrives today. He obviously did something right in the beginning. The second thing that came to mind was that even though Franklin is dead, decisions he made and actions he took while alive are still having an impact today! I thought to myself, "Now, *that's* a legacy!"

Evangelist Tony Campolo's organization conducted a study in the 1980's. They asked senior citizens one question: "If you could live your life all over again, what would you do differently?" The three most common responses were:

1. They would take time to reflect more frequently.

2. They would take more risks.

3. They would devote their lives to something that outlasts their own lifetimes.

Our society celebrates the achievements of athletes by immortalizing them in halls of fame. Once a year, a relative handful of motion-picture professionals go down in history when they hear their name mentioned at the end of the phrase, "And the Oscar goes to…"

People spend a lifetime trying to make their mark during their brief moments on the earth. Some spend thousands of hours and much money trying to become the first to find a cure for a particular disease or to be the first to accomplish some other noteworthy feat. Yet many miss the most natural opportunity to launch a world-changing legacy via their marriage. Most people fail to see the potential impact that a thriving, enduring marriage can have on the earth.

To get a perspective on the heart of God regarding legacy, the Book of Exodus offers a glimpse into the ripple effect of a righteous marriage.

> For I, the Lord your God, am a jealous God, punishing the children for the sin of the fathers to the third and fourth generation of those who hate me, but showing love to a thousand generations of those who love me and keep my commandments.
>
> —Ex. 20:5–6

Two principles are evident in this passage. First, God is more interested in blessing people than punishing them. This scripture's ratio of blessings-to-curses proves it. Those who hate the Lord will indeed be responsible for opening the door to punishment on their third and fourth generations after them. But compare that to a thousand generations of blessings lined up for those who love Him and keep His commandments!

Secondly, this Scripture gives the believer opportunity to affect the future beyond their own lifetime! Let's break it down. "…a thousand generations of those who love me and keep my commandments." Although the term *marriage* isn't overtly mentioned in this passage, the implied understanding is that the only way a person can have "generations" credited to them is by having children. Without referencing every Scripture that supports the institution of marriage versus fornication and adultery, marriage is the biblically prescribed environment to launch a legacy that invites the blessing promised in the Exodus passage.

As a professional filmmaker, I can honestly say that if I had to choose between winning an Academy Award for best director or being guaranteed that one hundred years from now, someone in my lineage will know the favor of God because I love Him today, I choose the latter!

Few brides and grooms give sober thought to the fact that their union could possibly be about much more than the "goo" they feel for one another. American society puts a premium on the individual and finding one's "personal destiny." It is mostly about "me" and "now."

In a recent TV interview, a famous international rock star talked about how, in spite of all the fame and money, the thing he regrets most is never having children. He hinted at how the notion of his own mortality becomes more real the older he gets. (He's currently in his mid-sixties.) It's only now that he is beginning to realize there is no one to pass his dreams along to, no one he cares about to pass on the wealth he has accumulated, no one to perpetuate what he believes in.

No matter what your upbringing was like, if you have committed your life to Jesus Christ and you are dedicated to growing every day in your personal faith and discipleship, you are a candidate to be what I call a Legacy Launcher! That is the beauty of rebirth. God designed a way that no matter what kind of dysfunctional, sin-riddled situation you may come from, if you truly love and live for Him, the living God promises to bless a thousand generations of your lineage!

From the age of twenty to age thirty, I was a missionary serving in Hong Kong with Youth With A Mission (YWAM). Although I was more of an itinerant missionary, traveling to more than twenty different countries on short-term, evangelistic outreaches, Hong Kong was home for me. I only learned enough Cantonese (the regional Chinese dialect) to give taxi directions and to keep from being cheated when shopping amongst the street merchants. I made several Chinese friends over the years, Christian and non-Christian. One of the strengths of the Chinese culture is that family heritage is highly valued, and there is a pervasive sense of patience. It's a kind of patience that America's two-hundred-year-old culture might be too young to deeply appreciate. It seems to be a patience, or confidence, in the future that stands on thousands of years of history.

Once, a Chinese friend told me an ancient adage that goes something like this:

> If I don't get you, my son will get you. If he doesn't get you, his son will get you. And if he doesn't get you, his son will get you, but one way or another, I'm gonna get you.

Now, I realize that can sound a bit vindictive, but if there's anything redemptive about this mind-set, it is reflected in the sense that this kind of culture understands and perpetuates strong links between the present, the past, and the future. Imagine what might happen if the people of God would be more forward thinking and would take up an attitude like this:

> If I don't bless you, my son will bless you. And if he doesn't bless you…one way or another, I'm going to bless you!

I grew up in a modest, loving household where my mother and father did the best they could to raise my younger brother and me. In the spring of 1978, my father had a dramatic, sovereign, life-changing encounter with Jesus Christ. His conversion happened without any church services, altar calls, television preachers, or gospel tracts. He simply picked up the Bible on the coffee table (which was only there as decoration) and began to thumb through it. He had tried reading the Bible before, but he couldn't understand it. This particular weekend was different. The Spirit of God fell upon him in a sovereign way, and not only could he understand everything he read over the next several hours, but the Lord personally led him in the sinner's prayer.

At first we thought Dad was simply suffering from a temporary chemical imbalance in his brain or some such thing. We were convinced that all this talk of love, God, and having found the real meaning of life would go away and he would eventually be back to normal. I'm glad we were wrong.

The funny thing about all this was that, of my whole family, my dad was the least religious. We went to church (which was more like a weekly social, community event in our minds than something that was part of our Monday through Saturday experience). I can say there was a healthy respect for God at home, which would often lead us to whisper a quickie prayer on icy roads or bless our morning bowl of cereal before diving in. But the only points we figured Dad was eligible for in heaven was being the first one to the car after church so we could get home in time to see the opening kickoff of the Redskins football game!

About six months after Pop's conversion, it was clear that not only was Jesus alive, but He could live in and change the lives of human beings. My father was truly a new creation.

Mom, my brother, Keith, and I eventually came to the conclusion that we could adjust to having a religious fanatic

Cool fact

in the house. (By the way, if you look up the word *fanatic* in a good dictionary, you'll find that it comes from a Latin root word *fanactus,* meaning "lover of God." If that's what a "fanatic" is, count me in!) But things really started getting shaken up when Dad found this Scripture in Acts:

> Believe in the Lord Jesus, and you will be saved—you and your household.
>
> —ACTS 16:31

Now, it would seem that heaven's sights were trained on the remaining three lost sheep of the Jackson household. Without forcing the matter, Dad made it clear that his number-one priority in life had now become to unleash a relentless battery of prayer missiles on the kingdom of darkness for the souls of every family member in his reach.

Almost twelve months to the date of my father's conversion, circumstances in my own life, as a high-school teen trying to find his way in the world, began to corner me. All this was happening without any manipulation by my father. The most logical conclusion I came to was that I should begin searching for God myself. Make no mistake. My father's indirect influence on me, just by his quietly changing lifestyle, had a profound impact on my inclination to believe God might really be there and be able to intervene in my personal life. When I saw Dad genuinely loving his enemies, turning the other cheek, and joyfully, immediately, and entirely releasing vices that had gripped his life for years, I knew someone stronger and bigger than any of us was at work in his life. Maybe He could also come into my life.

On April 22, 1979, I gave my life to Jesus with radical abandon. Now there were two family members praying for the remaining two to see the Light.

It would take another whole book to spell out the details, but a few months later, after a dramatic, almost tangible deliverance event that all four of us experienced, my brother and mother almost outran each other to surrender their lives to Christ on the same day!

Only thirty years or so have gone by since my father launched his legacy by dedicating his life to the Lord, but here's a cursory glance at what's happened since then, just in the arena of education and academics, for example:

1. My dad is a simple, wise man. He never went to high school but entered the workforce with only an eighth-grade education. He retired after more than thirty years of faithful employment with the city of Fairfax, Virginia's sanitation department.

2. About two years after I graduated from high school, the Lord placed me into one of the largest Christian mission organizations in the world (YWAM), where I met my life partner in this legacy-building adventure, Maria from Korea!

3. Maria earned her associate's degree before joining YWAM's mission work even before I met the Lord. "He who finds a wife finds a good thing, and obtains favor from the Lord" (Prov. 18:22, NKJV). (By the way, I don't believe the Bible is referring to women as inanimate objects here with the word *thing*. It's more like saying it's a "good thing" to be in this kind of relationship.)

4. By God's grace, I was able to earn a master's degree on a full scholarship at what is one of the world's premiere Christian graduate institutions, Regent University.

5. All three of our children have been identified as gifted by the state's public-school standards. They each rank in the upper percentiles of national standardized tests.

6. Our oldest son, David, was a recipient of the President's Award (George W. Bush) for Outstanding Academic Excellence for his scholastic achievement in his final year of elementary school and was subsequently enrolled in one of our city's three specialized academy programs for gifted students his age.

7. Our daughter, Mia, was selected to participate in the arts program of another of the three schools for the gifted and talented.

8. Our youngest son, Micah, loves the Lord and seems to be a magnet for the favor of God, in a similar way the Bible says Jesus grew in wisdom, stature, and favor with God and man.

None of these details are shared for boastful purposes, but rather to illustrate just a glimpse into what God can begin to do in the lineage of a redeemed man or woman of God.

The final twenty-five years of my parents' forty-four-year marriage, up to my mother's last breath, provides me and my children with a viable, indelible example that (a) it is truly possible to live "happily ever after" with one spouse for a lifetime, and (b) God is true to His Word, which promises blessings for a millennia to those who love Him.

One of the best ways you can prepare for marriage is to begin praying for your spouse now, especially if you are not seeing anyone at the moment. You might even want to do like my friend, Steve, and I did one evening. In my early days in the

Pray every day.

faith, God gave me the opportunity to fellowship with several young men of God. Steve and I would often sit for prolonged periods of time, either in his truck or my rusty old Volkswagen bug, praying.

One evening at Steve's parents' house, we felt a strong urge to pray for our future spouses. There were no prospects on the horizon at the time (which probably helped our prayers be more about what God wanted us to pray than what we wanted). By the time our prayer time ended, we knew that two women of God somewhere in the world were indeed blessed!

If you are single, try it sometime. You'll find it to be one of the most invigorating prayer meetings you've ever experienced. If you need "starter fluid," here are some things you might consider praying for your future spouse:

+ Pray that he or she will be protected from being distracted by the wrong relationships.

+ Ask God to guide him or her into the healing of any broken relationships with his or her immediate family.

+ Ask the Lord to lead you in how to pray for your posterity.

+ Pray for him or her to develop such an insatiable hunger and thirst for God that even when they "find" you, they will continue to love the Lord more than they love you.

+ Ask God to clearly guide them regarding their education and career path.

+ Ask the Lord to not allow you to miss him or her, or to ever settle for anything but the right one He has for you. (A word of caution here: Once you've chosen and you've said "I do," then *do!* I know of married Christian men who have abandoned their wives and children, based on a distorted attitude that they "made a mistake" and "married the wrong person." Sorry, fella. "I do" means "you'd better!")

One of the best gifts you can give your marriage partner is to be able to share with them someday that you frequently prayed for them. What better way to lay a firm foundation for a marriage that goes the distance and a legacy that goes beyond your own lifetime than by praying prayers of faith for the special one God has for you?

3

Prepare to Join Each Other's Extended Families

IN CHAPTER I, the purpose was to get us thinking forward. The focus there was on the question, "What are the future possibilities of this glorious union between me and the spouse the Lord gives me?"

It usually only takes me about thirty seconds in conversation with a love-struck, engaged person to determine that the sum total of what they are focused on is "the big day." The ring, the cake, the tux, the dress, the flowers, the invitations, the photographer, the honeymoon destination, the church, the daddy-daughter dance, the unity candle thing—which never works, by the way. Why do people insist on trying to light a unity candle at every Christian wedding? The wick is always too short. The lighter never works. Even indoors, it seems like the wind is always blowing! Just a question; I digress.

Although these are valuable components of that wonderful day, once the sun sets on the grand event, what are you going to do to maximize the possibilities ahead? It is possible to have answers to that question before you even meet the right one.

In this chapter, we're looking back. We're asking the question, "What am I bringing into marriage (spiritually, emotionally, physically, economically, socially, habitually, inheritance)?" In other words, if you're a man, she's going to want to know what comes with the package. People in love get married every day without giving the slightest thought to each other's individual family traditions, family history, skeletons, debts, and so on.

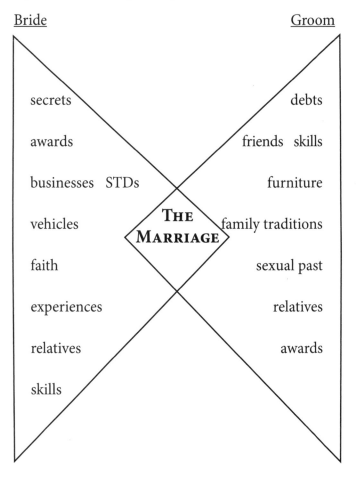

Bride   Groom

secrets   debts

awards   friends skills

businesses STDs   furniture

vehicles   **THE MARRIAGE**   family traditions

faith   sexual past

experiences   relatives

relatives   awards

skills

It's about more than just two lovers who finally get to live together legally and biblically. I tell people whom we advise prior to engagement, and even engaged couples, that marriage is the cross-pollination of two family trees. Whether you realize it or not, generations of blessings and curses converge when the two of you come together. One of the most loving things you can do for your future spouse is to get free, healed, and delivered (ideally, before you even get involved with anybody). It's not just about you two and the "goo." You and your spouse-to-be are spearheading two families coming together.

Before Maria and I became significant in each others' lives, we knew one another but were both involved in slightly more than platonic relationships with other people, who were also part of our missionary community. Ironically, the young lady I was spending time getting to know was also a good personal friend of Maria's. For privacy purposes, we'll call her Sarah.

Sarah and I were very attracted to each other on an emotional level. Yet there were some significant familial roadblocks that I am convinced would have been nearly impossible for us to successfully overcome had we continued to pursue a life together. I already mentioned the fact that my upbringing was simple. Much of my childhood was spent in a one-bedroom apartment with my low- to middle-income family. Sarah was from a significantly different economic background, as well as a completely different culture from my own.

Some would say, "But if you're truly in love, isn't that the most important thing?" Although every couple will have hurdles along the way, why put yourself and someone else in a position where there are more hurdles to clear than need be? While this will be covered in depth later, it comes down to who we "allow" ourselves to fall in love with. Opposites may attract, but there is something to be said for the idea of compatibility. I am suggesting that there is more to compatibility than whether or not we have chemistry. The more compatible your families are, the less stress there might be between the two of you over the long term.

The hit movie *My Big Fat Greek Wedding* was a lighthearted illustration of how two people from very different backgrounds proved their love for one another by respecting and embracing even the unlovely aspects of each other's families and cultures.

Maria and I, being an interracial couple, got to know many similar couples over the years. I'm reminded of one family where the husband is Caucasian American and his wife is Korean. He hated Korean food and would never so much as tolerate the smell of it in their home. He might as well have told her he didn't like her face or the size of her feet. For many Koreans, their traditional food is a connection with the essence of who they are.

Maria and I are often asked how we came together. Oddly enough, it was a meal that sealed the deal.

Let's face it. It's not every day that an African-American guy from Virginia gets engaged to a gal from Seoul, South Korea. In many ways, those two worlds couldn't be further apart. Shortly after falling in love with each other (September of '86), Maria and I decided to get married soon after (February of '87). Our missionary friends from around the world were excited and supportive of our decision. My family was thrilled that I had found the girl of my dreams, no matter where she came from. But the reaction from Maria's family indicated there might be some rough seas ahead.

Maria's father had passed away several years prior, so it was her older sister and her mother whom I would need to win over for her hand—daunting task, at best.

"Are you crazy?" was the mild translation of Hyun Sook's (Maria's sister) challenge to her baby sister during the first phone call after receiving our wedding invitation in the mail. Maria and I were planning to marry in Hong Kong, since that's where most of our mutual friends were. Unfortunately, a wedding in Hong Kong would be too far away for either of our families to attend. At the prompting of a wise friend and YWAM leader, Gary Stephens, we felt it would be important to respect Maria's mother and sister by my paying them a visit to Korea and giving them opportunity to object face to face or accept and support the idea of our marriage. As we prayed about the visit, we both sensed a nudging from God that I should go alone. Maria would wait (anxiously), praying and fasting in Hong Kong.

Arrangements were made for me to be met at Kimpo Airport in Seoul by Maria's family pastor, along with a dear Korean friend who spoke English well and would be able to interpret our conversations. From the moment I emerged through the jetway to the end of the taxi ride, which would take me to the location of meeting my potential future in-laws, Pastor Kim tried to prepare me for the worst. "Are you hungry?" he asked. The fact is, for some reason, I was starving. I was privately enjoying a certain amount of optimism that since Korean food is one of my favorite cuisines in the world, that would be at least one thing in my favor.

As we walked into the restaurant, I saw two ladies that I recognized from photographs Maria had shown me ducking their heads around the corner at first sight of my tiny entourage and me. Once we rounded the same corner and there was no place else for them to hide, they cautiously, yet politely, extended their hands in greeting. Miss Yoon, our translating friend, played the perfect neutral role as we batted small talk back and forth. Pastor Kim ordered all the dishes we would be sharing for lunch. I was concerned that the roaring of my stomach might be interpreted as nervousness, but in fact I was genuinely hungry.

After a few moments of awkward silence, the cross-examination began. Maria's sister started volleying what seemed to be a well-prepared and endless series of questions at me, ranging from what my plan would be for earning money to what my father did for a living. Although my Korean isn't the best, I can tell when someone is feeling passionate about something, and Hyun Sook was truly hot about this whole proposition. Fortunately, I was adept at applying a familiar passage of Scripture whenever I faced these kinds of heated situations:

A soft answer turns away wrath.

—PROVERBS 15:1, NKJV

It's a delicate balance you have to walk when being grilled by your potential in-laws. You don't want to come across as arrogant, yet you need to demonstrate a certain amount of conviction in the position you've taken. When in doubt, pray under your breath!

At last! The food arrived. After a fairly lengthy prayer by Pastor Kim, it was finally time to eat. What Maria's family didn't realize was that I had spent about a month in Korea three years prior, so I knew all the foods by name, and I knew what to eat first and what to eat next. I knew what sauces went with what dish. But what they seemed most impressed with was how proficient I was with the skinny, metal chopsticks Korea is famous for.

"You really know how to use chopsticks quite well. Where did you learn that?" The real answer to that question is that during my senior year in high school, I used to skip my afternoon classes on Fridays and go to a Chinese restaurant with my girlfriend because I got paid the day before from bagging groceries at the local supermarket. Somehow, I didn't feel like that would be the most appropriate answer. The fact that I had spent a month in Korea on a mission trip three years earlier might be a more appropriate answer.

Maria's sister took a breather on the question-and-answer session when she saw how serious I was about putting away some lunch. Once the meal was over, there were only one or two more questions. They seemed to have run out of ammunition. Now it was my turn.

"Now, I have a question for you," I said, making eye contact with Hyun Sook directly, since, in Korean culture, it's impolite for a younger person to make uninvited, direct eye contact with someone Maria's mother's age. Hyun Sook seemed a bit surprised that I would turn the tables like this, since I had been the one in the hot seat.

"Will you be my sister-in-law?" I asked.

Being the sharp lady that she is, she snapped back with a reply that basically, when translated, means, "Of course I'm going to be your sister-in-law. You're marrying my sister, aren't you?" I said, "No. If you don't want to be my sister-in-law, then I won't marry your sister. It's up to you."

The fact is, my question was not a ploy, or a bluff. I loved Maria more than anything in the world, and I wanted nothing more than to make her my wife, but I also knew that if her marrying me would mean lifelong tension and friction between us and her family, I loved her far too much to put her and us through that kind of grief. The ball was entirely in Sister and Mother's court.

The future and whether or not I would launch a legacy with Maria would be determined by her sister's next words. Pastor Kim got noticeably still. The interpreter even seemed a little uncomfortable, as if wondering where this could possibly go. Hyun Sook looked straight into my eyes, as if taking one final survey to detect the slightest glimpse of guile.

"Yes. I'll be your sister-in-law," she softly said, with a slight welcome-to-the-family smile. From that moment on, blessing and joy would be the best way to describe our relationship. We walked out of the same restaurant arm in arm! I spent the remaining day or two with my future in-laws taking me shopping for clothes and jewelry. They loaded me down with Maria's favorite Korean food and apologized for not being able to shower me with more material goods. What they did not realize was that they had given me the most valuable gift I could have dreamed of—their acceptance and respect.

I was having so much fun with my new "family" that I forgot to call Maria, who was fasting and praying in Hong Kong, to tell her the amazing happenings. Her most recent communication was her sister yelling over the phone about how crazy it was to be marrying a black man. I later learned that Maria had secretly made up her mind that once we were together again, if the first thing out of my mouth was anything other than, "You're not going to believe what happened—it was awesome," she was going to call the whole thing off herself.

When Maria met me at the airport in Hong Kong, she almost couldn't see me because I was laden with bags full of gifts from her family.

"How was it?" she asked.

I was so overwhelmed by the grace of God that I could hardly speak. "You're not going to believe what happened, Maria. It was awesome!"

As you grow closer to the one God has for you, always remember that more is coming together than the two of you alone. In many ways, whole families come together. In some cases, that's a blessing. Other times, it could prove to be an endless burden. Guard your heart. Proceed with caution. You may find yourself entangled with family pressures that you were not prepared for. Ideally, get to know the circumstances around your potential partner's family relationships before allowing yourselves to become overly entangled emotionally.

Before Maria and I were engaged, I knew that, culturally speaking, some day we would need to invite her mother to come and live her senior years with us. I understood that in Korean culture, nursing homes and retirement villages were not the way Korean families take care of their parents in the latter years of their lives.

I am blessed to be able to say that Maria's mother living with us for what turned out to be her final two years on this earth were two of the richest years of my life.

4

Promises, Vows, and *Other Forgotten Values*

S I MENTIONED previously, my parents' marriage lasted forty-four years before my mother's untimely death. By today's standards, that's almost miraculous! Mom and Dad married relatively young with very little money and no major fanfare. In stark contrast with the kinds of flamboyant wedding productions the rich and famous are known to put on, my parents simply planned one day to get together with a minister during their respective lunch breaks from work. After a brief exchange of vows, with the minister's wife serving as a witness, it was a quick kiss and back to work they went. No flowers, no rings, and no exotic honeymoon destinations. Just a simple promise taken seriously and, ultimately, lived out for a lifetime.

I would love to report that it was forty-four years of blissful tranquility between Mom and Dad. But before they met Jesus, there were plenty of challenges to the union, from outside the marriage and within. Doors were slammed. Sometimes harsh words soared through the house like javelins. Occasional threats of separation, even in my mind, seemed like the only feasible solution. In spite of the list of logical reasons to throw in the towel on their marriage, something deep in the bedrock of their individual value systems shouted, "No!" Although the songs of popular culture were reinforcing everything inside them that said "The Thrill is Gone," they had made a promise. They had made a vow.

In the late fifties and prior, the average person would rather suffer bodily harm than give a moment's thought to going back or his word.

In this chapter, my intention is to expose some subtle cultural trends that I believe are responsible for our society's diminishing ability to commit to *anything*, not to mention something that requires a lifelong commitment like marriage.

We are all familiar with the illustration of the frog in the pot of water. A (hypothetical) frog splashes happily around in the cool, refreshing, familiar environment. Theoretically (for the sake of all the helpless frogs in the world, I'm not recommending that anyone test this theory), if one were to drop a frog into a pot of boiling water, it would be expected to leap out immediately, instinctively aware that there is something wrong with the environment. But if you gradually turned up the heat on the happy critter swimming around in the comfortable water, it may not notice the slowly increasing temperature, eventually costing the poor thing its very life.

Guess what? The heat is on, and we are almost cooked when it comes to the unraveling of the fabric of our society, (i.e., marriage). Divorce statistics in the church are running neck and neck with the world. Why?

When financial analysts observe fluctuations in the value of a given index, they make recommendations for action to be taken in order to avoid a market crash. If only we as Christians, in our journeys toward marriage, could be so wise. We are sleeping through a cultural earthquake. Compared to the good old days, the collective character of our current society assigns little or no value to promises and vows. Consider the following cultural environment, and notice how it does not discriminate between sinners and saints. Everywhere we turn, there are myriad choices and options. If you don't like the thing or situation you are currently in, simply change to one that looks better. (Notice I did not say one that *is* better.) Car, job, school, toothbrush, Internet service provider, church, shoes, multiplex cinemas, computers, TV channels (cable, broadcast, satellite), food courts, and competing gas stations right next door to each other all provide us with ever-available options, choices, and opportunities to switch, swap, and bail out of whatever we may have "committed" to.

Professional athletes are advised by their greedy agents to bounce from team to team in search of bigger and better contracts and endorsements. Today, sports fans find themselves needing to be more loyal to logos or mascots than to human beings.

Nearly every commitment in the world can easily be slipped into and out of these days. The Devil has conveniently inserted the term *prenuptial agreement* into the legal language of marriage so couples can rest assured there is always a back door. Yet the Bible encourages us to commit to one spouse for a lifetime. Unfortunately, we hardly have any opportunity to practice commitment of any kind. How on earth can we expect to keep a lifelong promise to a person, no matter how much we feel like we love them? Our society conditions us, like the frog in the slowly boiling water, to develop a mind-set that quitting is to be expected.

Botox, silicone implants, and porcelain veneers (although wonderfully useful to people requiring reconstructive and cosmetic help to overcome birth defects and severe physical injury) mean we are no longer "stuck with" the looks we were born with. Science has even made a way for us to choose an alternate gender for ourselves if we wish! We worship choice and prioritize our right to personal happiness, regardless of how it impacts anyone else.

For illustration purposes, let's consider a major change that has taken place in the consumer/retailer arena. Forty years ago, if I bought a bag of potato chips, opened it up, and discovered it was barbecue but I wanted plain, taking the bag back and asking for a refund would have been laughable. I would have to make the best of the choice I made. The marketplace culture said, "All sales are final." Today in America, a different culture is commonplace. If you were to buy a toothbrush from Wal-Mart this afternoon, take it home and use it, but find that you can't quite get used to the grip, as long as you still have your receipt, you can take it back to customer service tomorrow and get your money back.

American retailers budget for two multibillion dollar spikes and dips in their annual cash flow in December:

+ A few days before Christmas, and
+ A few days after, when all the returns are expected.

So what can you do to strengthen your ability to commit? Is there a way to increase your chances of enjoying a lasting, successful marriage for a lifetime? I confidently propose the answer is yes. If you run out of time to finish this book, do yourself a favor and, at the very least, set your heart to applying the following tips, starting today:

+ Eliminate casual commitments and promises.
+ Develop the habit of keeping the commitments and promises you make (even at personal cost to you!).

How do we do this? First of all, we must watch our tongue. The Book of James tells us that our tongue gets us into all kinds of trouble. At the end of this chapter, I give a list of scriptures that you might consider spending serious time reading and meditating on.

Have you ever run into someone you haven't seen in a while and said something like, "Hey, let's get together some time"? Or what about, "I'll call you"? Months go by and neither you nor your friend make any effort to actually do what you said with your mouth. That was a casual commitment.

The great thing about having children is that you can always count on them to help you practice your promise-keeping skills! That must have been part of God's design for families.

I have three kids, and I'm finding that it's important to them that we establish certain family traditions. I don't mean cramming fruitcake down their throats at Christmas or forcing them to do things that only I enjoy. What they really seem to look forward to are age markers. The first right of passage for my kids was what we called their "apprenticeship year." We promised each child that at the age of eight, they would be able to go on at least one business or mission trip with Dad—just the two of us. They get to check us in at the airport. While we're on the trip, they get to help me pack the suitcases, pay for lunch, and even tip the waitress. Actually, for the whole year they get to be Daddy's right-hand helper. This would be our special bonding time, and I would teach them practical things in various areas of life.

When my youngest, Micah, was still only seven years old, he really looked forward to that mysterious year that he had seen his older brother and sister enjoy.

"Mike (as I often call him)," I said, "the next trip I go on, you're going with me." His eyes got big. He was almost ready to pack that very minute, even though I had no idea when or where my next trip would be. Because I'm a freelance film and TV producer/director, occasionally I got enough expense cash in per-diem funds that I could afford to use some of that money to buy a child's air ticket.

A few weeks later, I was booked on a trip to Canada, but this time I didn't have enough money to take Micah along. For his apprenticeship year, his brother, David, had been with me to shoot a video project in Tanzania, East Africa. His older sister, Mia, went with me for ten days to Japan, along with our church's gospel choir. Micah had yet to go anyplace with me, just the two of us.

Before I even mentioned to Micah that I was going on this trip, I racked my brain to find a way to afford to take him with me. Nevertheless, it was not going to happen. It looked as if I was going to have to go back on my word. I kept hearing my own teaching ringing in my ears: "Eliminate casual commitments, and keep the commitments you make." Concurrently, the world around me seemed to be shouting, "Don't worry about it. He's just a kid. He'll get over it."

As a last resort, I decided I would put Micah's ticket on our overburdened credit card if no other alternative became clear. Although that would put me in even more of a financial corner, I couldn't go back on my word to my son. Our children's perception of the faithfulness of God is modeled by our faithfulness to them.

I called Micah aside one evening, and we had a man-to-man talk about my next trip. I would simultaneously reveal my schedule and my dilemma to him. As I spelled out the challenges involved with trying to take him on my trip to Canada, his piercing black eyes showed no signs of loosening his hold on my promise. Then an idea came to mind. Maybe he would be willing to consider an exchange for something of equal value. I wasn't trying to pull a fast one on my son. I was trapped by unforeseen circumstances. Proverbs 6:2–4 says, "If you've been trapped by what you said, ensnared by the words of your mouth, then do this, my son, to free yourself. . . . Go—to the point of exhaustion—and give your neighbor no rest! Allow no sleep to your eyes, no slumber to your eyelids."

Hopefully you are able to observe more in the Proverbs passage than a loophole for getting out of commitments. If you look below the surface, you will find an implied understanding and basic principle of Christian discipleship, which is:

Our words are binding. The reason others should be able to take what we say seriously is that, over time, they witness us keeping our word, and those closest to us can confirm that the times are rare that we do something other than what we said we would do.

For Micah, the value was not in the distance of the trip or even the number of days away. The value was in being able to go someplace with Dad—just the two of us, which is actually something we had never really done since he was born.

We came to an arrangement. The day before I would fly out to Canada, Micah and I would drive up to Washington, DC together (about a four-hour drive, one way, from our home in Virginia at the time). We would have lunch together, visit the White House, the Washington Monument, and the Capitol building. We would watch the airplanes take off and land at Ronald Reagan International Airport. Before he would shake on the deal, there would be one final condition:

"Will we be able to get some French fries at McDonalds?" he pleaded.

It was a lovely, memorable day with my little boy. Even though it was a few years ago now, he often brings it up with fond memories.

It would have been easier to simply say, "Oops Mike, I can't take you this time. Sorry, Son." I could have promised to bring him something back from my trip to Canada. Although he might have appreciated the gift, he would not have perceived it as something of equal value to going with me. In many ways, the DC trip was a greater joy to me than bringing something back from Canada would have been. That's why the writer of Proverbs contends that the value of our word is worth losing sleep to protect!

The challenge to all of us is to stop developing skill in taking the easy way out of our commitments and to do everything possible to honor those promises. The lifelong commitment of marriage is fulfilled one promise, one day at a time.

Restoration and Restitution

Are we perfect? No. Are we going to sometimes have to do something other than what we've promised? Occasionally. Here are two practical ways to exercise promise keeping.

1. Ask the Lord to point out promises you may have made and not kept.

If He shows you something, commit to God that you will do your best to make it right, no matter how much time has passed. Outline an action plan to restore and make restitution ASAP.

Here is an example from my own life. My very first car cost me $100. It was a simple Chevy station wagon with a small engine that ran well. Like many sixteen-year-olds in my town, what my car looked like really mattered. I painted the muddy brown thing a sapphire black and put pinstripe flames on the doors. I even tinted the rear windows with that plastic stuff that always reveals its cheapness by bubbling up after a few days! The final touch was racing tires with white raised lettering on the sidewalls. The hot tires would be all I needed to cruise the boulevard with pride. The only problem was, I could not afford the cool tires on my minimum-wage evening job at the grocery store.

Trying to teach me responsibility while helping me finish off my dreamboat, my dad loaned me the $160 I needed for the tires. He made it very clear that this was a loan and not a gift. Years and years went by (more than twenty, to be exact) before I realized one day that I had never paid my father back for the tires that I agreed were supplied to me as a loan.

I had forgotten about the tires. My father had long since forgotten about the tires and the $160. But there was Someone who did not forget about the tires or the money—the Holy Spirit. Wouldn't you know it that one day, twenty-some years later, I got a knock on my heart's door, and it was the Holy Spirit reminding me of my promise to my father.

I am convinced that our attitude toward these kinds of unwritten contracts has an impact on our present level of provision and blessing, whether we remember them or not.

After an intense internal battle with myself regarding what my next move would be, I decided to call Dad. I didn't even want to think about what twenty years of compounded interest on $160 would be! Regardless, it was time to make good on my word.

It took a while for Dad to connect with the memory of that distant agreement, but eventually he remembered. Like the great man of God that he is, he promptly and entirely released me of my obligation, with one stipulation, "When you get rich someday, you can pay me back then!" That was Dad's way of saying, "Don't bother."

2. Share your decision to exercise restitution with someone else.

Humbly verbalizing your action plan and promise provides added incentive to fulfill your vow. It is a form of accountability. By the way, this is why marriage ceremonies involve witnesses.

If you practice and exercise these skills in smaller, everyday commitments, you will become a person of integrity. You will also develop a reputation of being trustworthy. Then, when it comes to making the ultimate promise, second only to your commitment to Christ, you will have strengthened the promise "muscles" required to pull your weight in marriage.

Take time to meditate on a few familiar Scripture passages that remind us of what our attitude should be about the words that come out of our mouths:

+ Matthew 5:37
+ Matthew 12:36
+ Ecclesiastes 5:5
+ James 5:12

5

The Third Entity: Why God Hates Divorce

I REALIZE THAT THE second part of this chapter's title rubs a certain percent of my audience the wrong way. I would be tempted to take their rejection personally if the concept of God hating divorce was my idea, but it's not. It is in the Bible. Some readers may falter here by inferring, "Since God hates divorce, and (perhaps) I'm divorced, then God must hate me." Nothing could be further from the truth!

I do not pretend to be a Bible scholar, although many Bible scholars have indirectly mentored me. I submit to you that the spirit of the Scripture in question (Mal. 2:16, NAS), "'I hate divorce,' says the Lord God of Israel..." could be understood this way: "God hates what divorce does to people."

Most would agree that it is possible to simultaneously hate war yet love and support one's family members and friends who serve in the military, for example. Jesus's very death on the cross proved, once and for all, that it is possible to hate sin (no, I am not across-the-board categorizing divorce as sin) without hating those who commit sin.

This chapter is *not* an indictment against divorced people, but rather an attempt to help future couples avoid the traps and politically-correct lies that tend to lull many into believing that divorce is the only solution to solving marital conflict.

If your goal is to be a vital partner in a successful marriage that goes the distance, first you must evaluate your own philosophy of marriage and divorce. Everyone, whether they realize it or not, has a philosophy of marriage. Another term for it is *worldview*. What is your personal philosophy of marriage? The Bible says God has "written His laws on [our] hearts…" In other words, we all have a moral compass that we refer to, or ignore, when we make decisions of right and wrong, good and bad.

Here are seven simple but important questions that may help you figure out what your current philosophy of marriage is:

1. How many people constitute a marriage? (One, two, three? More?)

2. Should people get married? If so, why? If not, why not?

3. What is the purpose of marriage?

4. Why do people get married?

5. How will you know if and to whom you should get married?

6. Are there limits, in your mind, regarding age differences, gender, and blood relationship? If so, what are the limits? If not, why no limits?

7. When, if ever, is divorce appropriate? Why or why not?

Take some time to ponder the questions above, and write down your answers. Writing your answers helps clarify exactly what your worldview on the subject of marriage really is. It also gives you a frame of reference for the future. If you are going to be a legacy launcher, get in the habit of writing your thoughts down and filing them for easy future reference.

Imagine marrying someone whose answers to the seven questions above are completely opposite from yours. "But Kenny, we love each other." Yes. I call that "goo." Goo is OK, but as I'll discuss in chapter 7 on "A Marriage Fuel Gage," goo comes and goes. It cannot be relied on to sustain a marriage for a lifetime.

I am willing to go as far as to say, if you are serious about marrying someone even now but don't want to make a mistake in your decision, sit down with the person and "compare notes" (your answers to the seven questions above). If the two of you come to a major point of contention on either of the questions philosophically, you may need to slow down and get counsel. There are definitely some hairpin curves ahead!

Now, take your answers to the same seven questions and apply these follow-up questions to each of the answers you gave:

1. What outside influences helped you form your philosophy of marriage?

2. What does the Bible say?

There are many influences on our core value system. Observations of marriages during childhood, media images, friends, and authority figures seem to have the most impact on our philosophy of marriage.

THE THIRD ENTITY

The concept of the "third entity" has the potential to help you and your future marriage partner finish the race well or, as the storybooks say, "live happily ever after"!

The very first of the seven questions above is, "How many

people constitute a marriage? (One, two, three? More?)" Although one may choose to argue in favor of polygamy, my reading of the New Testament is that monogamy is recommended, not to mention that polygamy is illegal in most of the civilized world. On that basis, the remainder of this chapter—and book, for that matter—will be based on the position that the definition of marriage is a contractual and covenantal relationship between one man and one woman (i.e., two people). Yet, I propose, there is a third entity. Although most readers are about to jump to the conclusion that I am suggesting that God is the third entity, that is not who or what I am referring to in this instance.

The Microsoft Corporation is, in legal terms, an entity made up of people who have come together for a common purpose. The United States Congress is an entity. The presidency is an entity that changes hands in the US either every four years or every eight years, depending on the incumbent's electoral success. In business terms, companies must frequently evaluate the fiscal health of the business, as if it were a living thing. If expenses are outrunning income, the business can be said to be in poor financial health. If the people running the business do not act quickly enough and make good decisions, the business could die.

Every marriage is made up of three entities: you, your spouse, and the marriage. I often compare the third entity, or the marriage, to a brand-new baby. How it is treated and tended to in the early years will have a significant impact on how it turns out in later years.

Imagine two parents with a bouncing two-year-old. One morning, one of the parents notices a severe rash on the child's skin. The baby cries and cries, inconsolably, because of a high fever. The concerned parent rushes to the other parent, holding the screaming toddler, asking the preoccupied parent to call the doctor or to get ready to take the child for emergency care. But the other parent blows the situation off, as if the child doesn't even exist. "Can't you see I'm busy reading the newspaper right now?" the parent replies. "And do something about that noise, would ya?"

Would that not be the most absurd picture you could ever imagine? Unfortunately, that is exactly the way some married people treat their marriage. One partner notices the marriage is in trouble, but the other is unaware that this vital entity is having trouble breathing. Sometimes both of the two main entities choose to neglect the poor, helpless third entity as it gasps for breath, being smothered by things like selfishness, adultery, ridicule, secret sins, financial cares, lies, unforgiveness, and neglect.

Although I have forgotten most of what I learned in high school, for some reason there is one concept from science that has stuck with me all these years: matter can never completely be reduced to the point of nonexistence. It can change forms, but there will always be something there. While a marriage is not a thing we can perceive in the physical world, when two become one, there will always be something "there," even after a divorce. The third entity doesn't just disappear with the signing of a few legal papers. Like physical matter in the science world, the third entity just takes on another form in divorce. It lives on, but only as a wounded, injured, broken relationship. Yes, wounds can heal, but even though they are no longer painful, the ever presence of scars immortalizes a past of pain. No amount of closure or moving on can beautify the permanent scars the third entity now bears.

I know this is a radical perspective, but I can no longer sit back and watch 50 percent of Christian marriages in my generation unravel at the same pace as those who don't know God. We are losing the very foundations of our society. It must stop!

I bring a gentle reminder here that this book is not designed for divorced people. Some of my very best Christian friends in the world are divorced and remarried. If you are divorced and finding this material a bit difficult to swallow, keep in mind that it is meant to be preventative medicine. Birth control pills do not work for pregnant women! This sobering perspective on the gravity of divorce is designed to challenge and prepare Christian singles who have never been married before. My purposes are twofold:

1. To help Christian singles see how valuable marriage is before they take the plunge.

2. To provide Christian singles with a clear understanding of the value of what is being forfeited in divorce.

No doubt your own life has been touched by divorce in some way or another. Am I saying it is never right to get a divorce? Of course not. The Scriptures lay out clear grounds for divorce in the case of marital unfaithfulness. Despite how terribly painful that situation always is, there are documented stories of couples who have managed to even get beyond that and see their marriage and family fully restored.

My prayer for you is that you and the spouse that you allow the Lord to lead you to will always be willing to fight for the life of the third entity—your marriage.

6

Spiritual Warfare and Marriage

THIS CHAPTER IS probably the most distinguishing factor between this book and others available in the mainstream marketplace today. In order to fully benefit from all that these principles have to offer, there needs to be a foundation of faith in Jesus Christ. Jesus said, "Apart from me, you can do nothing" (John 15:5). Scripture also says, "For he who comes to God must believe that He is, and that He is a rewarder of those who diligently seek Him" (Heb. 11:6, NKJV). So, if someone is reading this book without even believing in God, the Devil, or the spiritual world, this chapter is really going to be a challenge, because now we're going to be talking about the Devil.

Unfortunately, some don't believe there is a real "enemy of our souls," even though God goes to great lengths in Scripture to remind us, over and over, that the Devil exists and his ultimate purpose is to kill, steal, and destroy. What better place to start analyzing our enemy's tactics against marriage relationships than in the Book of Genesis?

Just days into the creation event, one of the first characters we meet in the whole Bible is the Serpent (the Devil). Of all the possible things the Devil could have been doing in the earth, he zeroed in on what would have the most far-reaching, long-lasting impact, if he were to succeed. His mission? To destroy the very creation God had made. He also set out to ruin the first marriage. It was the Devil's attempt at getting back at God for tossing him out of heaven after his little "I will" speech (Isa. 14:13–14). The exact sin and death that Jesus had to suffer and die for was ushered into the world by the first couple, Adam and Eve (Gen. 2:20–3:24).

The first thing we see in this group of scriptures is that God is the One who initiated the union: "Then the Lord God made a woman from the rib he had taken out of the man, and he brought her to the man" (Gen 2:22). The number one spiritual warfare principle here is *let God do the picking.* In the good old days, ministers, when pronouncing that a new couple is now husband and wife, would say, "And what God has joined together, let not man put asunder." In our own day and time, sometimes the enemy is allowed to slip in right from the beginning if we rely on our own judgment and trust solely in our feelings rather than God to choose our life partner.

The next thing we learn from the first family is what I call domestic sovereignty: "That is why a man leaves his father and mother and is united to his wife, and they become one flesh" (Gen. 2:24). A quick side note here: God is *so smart!* He knew that one day our society would wrestle with crazy notions like same-sex marriage and sex-change operations, so in this one passage of Scripture He addresses it all: "A man will leave his father and mother..." Here, the gender distinctions are clear and non-confusing. The family in this case is not made up of two male domestic partners or two female domestic partners, but one father and one mother who produced at least this one son. Everyone knows their role, who they are, and where they came from. Now, this man who has been raised by a father and a mother will leave them and be united with a woman (not with another man), "and they two will become one flesh" (i.e., domestically sovereign). They become a unique family unit.

Wow! God is so smart! Really cool

One of the avenues the Devil takes in destroying marriages is to broker a compromise in domestic sovereignty. Some people, although married, continue to rely too heavily on close involvement with their mom and dad.

In one instance, I witnessed a couple, and ultimately their entire family, disintegrate. Not only did she remain emotionally attached to her parents, but the entire family of four moved in with her mom and dad without a definite departure date in mind. Whenever the husband and the wife had differences of opinion, which was just about nonstop, she would immediately confide in Mom and Dad, who were conveniently in the other room. By the time she, Mom, and Dad were finished ganging up on the husband, who should have been leading his own domestically sovereign household anyway, the marriage was over.

Genesis 2:25 states, "Adam and his wife were both naked, and they felt no shame." This portion of Scripture outlines two important components in the foundation of a marriage: intimacy and trust. Concurrently, they become two essential targets of the enemy of our souls.

Intimacy and Trust

Physical intimacy between a man and a woman is about much more than sex, and sex can be about more than physical gratification. Hollywood (although, vocationally, I am part of that industry) has done society a major disservice, to say the least, by reinforcing a culture of promiscuity. Hooking up, one-night stands, and such have become the norm, unfortunately, even among many Christians. The Bible calls it fornication. So what's wrong with casual sex? What does that have to do with one's future marriage relationship?

Safeguarded intimacy produces trust between a man and a woman. Where trust is uncompromised, there is unity. Unity, in kingdom of God terms, is a magnet for the blessings of God! (See Psalm 133:1–3.)

One man and one woman truly living in intimate unity is a spiritually powerful thing. Unfortunately, Adam and Eve's unified decision to follow the Devil's lead and disobey God was so significant that God's entire creation was altered as a result. It's called the fall of man. What is the aftermath of this first recorded marital casualty, in spiritual warfare terms? We still experience the impact of our first parents' inadvertent cooperation with Satan thousands of years ago:

- The Devil became the "prince of the power of the air" (Eph. 2:2, NKJV).

- Mankind could no longer walk and talk face-to-face with God because His glory and holiness would literally be too much for mankind's fallen flesh to handle. We would die! So, God is doing us a favor by concealing the fullness of Himself physically and visibly. Thank you, Lord!

- The woman would have to endure pain during childbirth.

- The ground was cursed.

- Man would have to work hard to survive.

- No one born from then on would live eternally (in the current physical condition we know now), but everyone would die someday, including Adam and Eve.

Thank God that His Son, Jesus, is our Redeemer! Because of His sacrifice on the cross and resurrection from the dead, it is possible that a godly marriage built on a foundation of righteousness (which comes from God, not our own efforts)

Amazing - thank you God!.

can know true intimacy and trust, resulting in the kind of unity where Jesus said, "They will have whatever they ask" (Matt. 18:19). I believe that means regularly answered prayer and victory over the works of the Devil. That's powerful!

So, if you were the Devil and you observed that unified prayer resulted in true intimacy and trust, what aspect of a marriage would you target?

I believe marriage was designed by God to be the nucleus of all human relationships on the earth. Not the church (though vital), the government, school systems, foster programs, boys and girls clubs, scouts, or any other way that people connect with each other can command the kind of blessing that a marriage can. Otherwise, when creation was under way, God would have produced several humans at a time and formed a corporation, or a network of churches, or some other form of efficient, human interaction. No. He started the whole human picture with a man and a woman in intimate relationship together.

Here is how it is supposed to work. Thriving, unified marriages produce offspring. Those children are trained "in the way they should go" (Prov. 22:6) by godly parents who lead them to faith in Christ and guide them into preserving their own gift of physical intimacy for their life partner. Together, the new domestically sovereign couple builds a truly intimate, trusting marriage equipped to repel the Devil's access in the earth. Members from those whole, blessed family units form another layer of relationship called the church, then cities make up nations.

What kind of a threat could strong, stable marriages be to the Devil's purposes? Even though the Bible says that in heaven there will be no marriage or giving in marriage (in other words, we shouldn't expect to be hanging out with our spouses in eternity), why is marriage such a big deal here on earth?

+ Marriage is a visible illustration and foretaste of Jesus's relationship with the bride of Christ (the church): "Husbands love your wives just as Christ loved the church" (Eph. 5:25).

+ Studies have demonstrated over and over that children raised in a loving, two-parent (mom and dad) environment tend to grow up as more stable adults than those who don't.

+ Assuming that a couple bears or adopts children, marriage is the ideal evangelism context for Christian couples. As parents, we have the privilege of shaping someone's disposition toward Jesus Christ every day from conception! "Train up a child in the way he should go, and when he is old he will not depart from it" (Prov. 22:6, NKJV). That is a biblical promise.

+ "How could one put a thousand to flight, and two put ten thousand to flight?" (Deut. 32:30).

A strong, stable marriage can have a serious impact on the enemy's purposes. Imagine a world full of lifelong marriages filled with the love and kingdom of God. What if the earth were populated with families made up of children living happy, normal lives with two loving parents that have blessed their growing-up years with all the resources they need to thrive and advance the purposes of God in the earth? It's a tall order, but it all starts with you and me learning how to engage in spiritual warfare—fighting for our marriages and our legacies.

Am I suggesting we strive to create a utopia on the earth? Not really. I think Jesus is working on that for us in heaven! Remember, He said He's "going to prepare a place" for us. I'm trying to do something easier than that. I want to spark the desire in you to position yourself spiritually to be part of a marriage that is blessed by God. This book is not a marriage repair kit. There are other books that do a better job at that than this can. I see this book as a kind of track-and-field coach. I want to see you and your running partner be as prepared as possible, not only to run the best race you can, but to win!

A fatalist looks at my scenario of the way things are supposed to be and throws up his hands when he compares that to the way things are. Rampant divorce, incest, gender confusion, abortion, internet pornography, and society's struggle with the definition of marriage itself all indicate that we fight an uphill battle. How could it possibly be won? One spiritually-equipped marriage at a time.

THE SPIRITUAL POWER OF PORNOGRAPHY

On September 11, 2001, an enemy whose plan went undetected attacked the United States of America. American spy entities, however, acknowledge that there was indeed an increase in surveillance "chatter" that indicated something was stirring. The problem was, they didn't know exactly who the enemy was or precisely what, when, or where the enemy planned to strike. This critical intelligence vacuum resulted in the largest single-day loss of American lives since Pearl Harbor.

The 9-11 terrorist attacks caused a kind of devastation that has had a ripple effect, not only in every sphere of American society, but the world. That is the exact kind of impact the Devil wants to have on the people of God—collateral damage, long-lasting, and far-reaching.

If my position is true, that marriage was designed by God to be the nucleus of all human relationships on the earth, then it should come as no surprise that our enemy keeps targeting marriages. Social science research seems to stop short at

hmm... interesting

53

pointing to a direct "causation" link between porn addiction and a Christian man's decision to be unfaithful in marriage. However, in her eye-opening book, *Pornified*, author Pamela Paul suggests that pornography is a significant player in the destruction of marriages as well as other important aspects of life. Remember, the Bible says, "The thief comes only to kill, steal, and destroy" (John 10:10).

One of the most heart-wrenching letters I ever received in my life was from the son of a friend of mine. The young, pre-teenaged son wrote, "Would you please talk to my father? I want him to come home…I need my father."

Where was the young boy's father? He was off, ensnared in his second adulterous affair. Neither his marriage, his family, nor his legacy were worth forfeiting the pleasure of sin for a season. Unfortunately, my friend's son joined the ranks of countless young boys being raised by a single mother. The marriage ended in divorce. From prior discussions together, the one thing that I know my friend was not able to break free from was pornography. All of that visual stimulation ignited desires that could not righteously be fulfilled.

In spiritual warfare terms, (especially men) consider pornography to be a sort of "boot camp" for adultery. It's where anyone who really wants to be a skillful adulterer goes for training. Jesus said if a man looks at a woman lustfully, he's committed adultery with her already in his heart (Matt, 5:28). Since pornography is predominantly experienced with the eyes, whether you know it or not, practice makes perfect.

Before I get into this sensitive subject in depth, allow me to admonish young women readers who are preparing for marriage. (Although addiction to pornography is not unique to males, proportionately, the porn industry targets men more than women.) Ladies, before you make a commitment to marry any man, be sure to put the question of pornography on the table of your premarital discussions together. Find a gracious way to inquire about your future husband's history and current disposition to porn.

This is another great opportunity for me to expose one of the enemy's lies! Before you drop the wedding invitations in the mail, you might find a non-threatening way to ask him something like this: "I've heard that there are some couples who actually use pornographic material as a means of 'enhancing' their love life. What do you think about that, Honey?"

I know, it's kind of a trick question (it's one of those wisdom-of-Solomon kinds of tests), but it might be the best way to be sure you are getting an uncensored answer. If his response indicates that he thinks it is a good idea and he even seems to be glad you appear to be open to the notion, I highly recommend you hold off on mailing out the invitations. Your guy may still be in bondage, and you do not want to start off a marriage with the Devil having that kind of spiritual access to your intimacy together. If he seems shocked and almost disappointed that you even asked such a thing, you can be somewhat confident that he walks in victory in that area of his life.

The reason this is so important, ladies, is that if your guy is battling this problem currently, he is unwittingly rehearsing adultery. Imagine a child swatting at a beehive as if it were a piñata. The kid is going to have a hard time trying to coax the bees to go back inside the hive once they've been stirred up!

In the same way, when someone allows pornography to trigger certain God-given, natural urges and drives in the wrong way at the wrong time, a spiritual cycle of lust-ungodly-gratification-guilt-lust-ungodly-gratification-guilt is set in motion. What makes it so difficult to break out of is that the cycle attaches itself to our God-given, perfectly natural sexual response system, which is designed to be cultivated and exercised in the intimacy of marriage.

I want to offer a perspective that can hopefully serve as a motivation to either stay far away from this pit or to seek freedom if you're already stuck in it. I submit that there are at least three major things that pornography does to men (with the understanding that it severely demeans women).

1. Pornography diminishes manhood.

How? By making a man a "slave" to lust. Foolishly, some men actually use pornography to introduce their sons to "the birds and the bees." That makes about as much sense as hiring a paroled pedophile to be the security guard at a children's daycare center!

Slavery of any kind, especially for Spirit-led, Christian men, strips a man of his self-esteem, his dignity, and his spiritual authority in the earth. Having been gloriously set free from the bondage of pornography myself, I speak with authority when I say that during the years that I struggled with this enemy, my Christian witness and spiritual authority were absolutely no threat to the Devil's kingdom. Guilt paralyzed me into either hopeless ineffectiveness or hypocrisy.

2. Pornography gradually poisons marriages.

Like any other organism, once a poison has entered the system, it can threaten the very life of the organism. Marriage is no different. If a married man's true manhood is deficient, he cannot be the man he needs to be to husband his wife. He is only able to partially fulfill his duties of spiritual leadership. He has been stripped of spiritual authority. (Hint to married women: If your Christian husband is reluctant to initiate family prayer meetings and Bible studies, it may not be just because he's tired. Pray fervently before confronting or talking with him about it. Ask the Lord to expose anything he may need to be freed up from in this area.)

I have known of some women who describe their husbands

as having suddenly become cold towards them, without explanation. I would not be surprised to discover that these men are dealing with a secret struggle that can be linked to exposure to pornography.

3. Pornography threatens potential legacies.

Remember, marriage is not just about you two and the "goo." You have the chance to build a foundation upon which subsequent generations from your marriage can change the world!

My final thought in this area is a revelation that the Lord used to set me free. I hope it can be a part of launching someone else into a life of freedom from so-called adult entertainment.

Matthew 6:22–23 (NKJV) says:

> The lamp of the body is the eye. If therefore your eye is good, your whole body will be full of light. But if your eye is bad, your whole body will be full of darkness. If therefore the light that is in you is darkness, how great *is* that darkness!

Again, I make no claims to being a theologian. Bible scholars do a much better job dissecting this passage than I can, hermeneutically and exegetically (which are fancy theological words that help Bible scholars feel smarter than the rest of us!). Nevertheless, when I approached this passage at face value, as opposed to immediately looking at it metaphorically, it shook me to the core. First of all, it is the way this scripture strikes me, as someone in the film and television profession. *Light* is our bread and butter. Basic photographic science is at the root of all film and television content. Cameras need light to work. Now, here comes the revelation (to thick people like me).

Light is physical. Jesus knew that light was physical centuries before scientists found a way to accurately measure the fact that light travels at a speed of 186,000 miles per second. That is why, in this passage of Scripture, He speaks of light in *physical* terms. We don't normally refer to the possibility of one's whole body being *filled with light*. Because that seems so odd, most readers probably shift into metaphor mode because they cannot reconcile this unusual teaching of Jesus. Yet because light is physical, the passage makes all the sense in the world.

It is difficult for us to think of light as physical because it is not tactile. We can't handle light with our hands. We can feel heat, but light is intangible. Nevertheless, it is physical. The smallest particle of light is known as a photon. Photons travel in a straight line. They bounce off the surface of objects in the material world, like trees, people's faces, computer screens, and magazines, and they travel toward our eyes. These little particles of matter enter our pupils, stimulating the rods and cones in our eyes (so now they are physically inside our body), which transmit an electrical signal to our brains, translating that signal into an image. The brain processes that image, and we consequently decide how we are going to respond to what we see.

The moment I realized that the process of vision means, in a sense, whatever I "see" is, in a small way, coming into my body, I was like a smoker at the autopsy of another smoker. Once you have seen the lungs of a smoker, compared with the lungs of a nonsmoker, to smoke or not to smoke becomes a no-brainer! At least it should.

Now I could gladly say with the psalmist, "I will set [intentionally place; on purpose; of my own volition] no wicked thing before my eyes" (Ps. 101:3, NKJV).

So, what are some weapons we can use to resist the Devil as we prepare for marriage? Read Ephesians 6, "the armor of God" passage, and 2 Corinthians 10:3–4, which says, "we do not wage war as the world does."

7

A Marriage Fuel Gauge

I WAS SIXTEEN WHEN I got my first car. Actually, I bought it when I was fifteen, but I had to wait twelve agonizing months until I turned the legal age to drive in my state. I wasn't very good with managing my massive McDonald's paycheck each week, so, almost like clockwork, I would find myself, the day before payday, having run out of gas someplace and needing to phone my Dad to come get me going again.

I suppose there are many reasons people's cars run out of gas. With me it was poor financial management. Others, I suppose, might run out because they fail to frequently monitor the fuel gauge. Others yet may find that they have miscalculated the estimated distance they can drive on the fuel they have remaining. If you have ever driven in the Southwestern part of the United States, you know that in some areas there are critically long distances between fueling stations as you drive across the desert. Fortunately that never happened to me. I could think of a few reasons not to run out of gas in the middle of the desert at night.

Recently, our family was blessed with the gift of a gently used minivan. It looks nice and drives very comfortably. There is only one tiny issue with the vehicle. Every now and then (about one out of every ten to fifteen starts), the fuel gauge malfunctions.

GET MARRIED for CHRIST'S SAKE

The needle sits on "E," and the amber-colored warning light comes on. The first time it happened, my wife called me from her cell phone and scolded me for not putting any fuel in the car. The odd thing was, I recall glancing at the fuel gauge just the night before on my way back home from my youngest son's soccer practice. The needle registered three-quarters of a tank full, and I had driven less than three miles. Had someone found a way to steal our gasoline during the night, right in our own driveway? That seemed very out of character for our quiet neighborhood.

Well, Maria made it safely to the gas station but was surprised when she went to fill up the tank. It reached the full level immediately, after only two or three gallons had been pumped. Because we know the capacity of the tank is much more than that, the only explanation had to be an electrical or mechanical fault between the fuel gauge and tank. This was confirmed a few days later when I was driving the vehicle myself.

Back to my adventuresome youth. Of all the ill-advised things I did and contemplated doing as a teenager, it never ever crossed my mind to throw away my car just because it had run out of fuel. No one ever needed to tell me that an empty gas tank is not a good enough reason to throw a car away. That would be ridiculous. The engine was in fine working order. All the tires (paid for by my dad) had plenty of life left in them. Structurally, the car was sound. Most important of all, some of the girls in my high school marching band thought the car was cool because of my tinted (bubble-riddled) back windows! The car was too valuable to get rid of just because the gas tank needed filling.

Unfortunately, that is exactly what thousands of people do every day when they decide to give up and walk away from their marriage.

There are five words in the English language that should never be used in sequence because together their meaning forms what, in my opinion, should be considered an oxymoron. We hear the phrase in popular songs, dialogue from Hollywood movie scripts, daytime soap operas, and romance novels: "I don't love you anymore."

Love is a rechargeable battery! It's a refillable fuel tank! But many people treat it like a one-time-use battery to be disposed of the first time its juice, or what I call the "goo," runs dry.

From middle school to high school and right through adulthood, people recklessly bounce from relationship to relationship with the false expectation that somewhere out there is the perfect human being with whom, once they connect, the "love tank" will never run dry.

When are we going to get it? One hundred-plus years of watching the wealthiest, prettiest, most talented couples in Hollywood has proven by their own high-profile, real-life love disasters that a lasting, vibrant marriage takes some effort.

Question: Is it possible to purchase a brand-new car and care for that car for up to twenty years and the car never once run out of fuel? Answer: yes. Running out of fuel is not inevitable. Nobody's car *has* to run out of gas. Just as during normal use of a vehicle fuel is spent, so it is in marriage. The love tank will Good go from full to empty as life goes on. Expect it. It is normal, no to remember matter what the tabloids tell you. Don't be surprised when you notice some day that your "goo factor" isn't the same as it was on the wedding day. Good news: it doesn't mean it's over! It simply means you need to find the nearest filling station.

Over the next few pages I want to introduce to you a tool that I hope will help you in your future marriage to be able to gauge the fuel level and give you some tips on how to fill the tank back up, over and over again.

DISCOVERY PHASE

I am confident that if you are an adult of average intelligence, you have experienced the fact that you have only one chance to make a first impression, whether it's a job interview or a blind date. First impressions come around only once. Consequently, when you meet someone who is a potential candidate for being your life partner (i.e., they are the appropriate gender and are legally and biblically single), in a matter of seconds that person receives a "score," if you will, the moment you mentally run them through what I call your subliminal first impression checklist (SFIC).

Not everyone has the same SFIC. Yours may include physical characteristics such as height, weight, hair color, eye color, apparent age, and other personal appearance factors. We also tend to evaluate people by certain intangible qualities such as their social graces, or lack thereof. We make mental notes that measure their trustworthiness. Believe it or not, you are in the early stages of what I like to call the *discovery phase*.

You may have several godly relationships with different people at the same time, such as in a church college and career group. Let's say that you have narrowed your options down to one person in whom you are most interested. The relationship progresses to the point where the two of you have communicated some level of mutual openness to allowing the relationship to go as far as it might (including marriage). In many cases, things tend to happen pretty fast at this point. Sometimes too fast for one of you (usually the guy!).

To use the car analogy again, it is no longer as if you are driving two different cars anymore. Now you are in the same car (i.e., the relationship), and there is only one fuel gauge, not two independent ones.

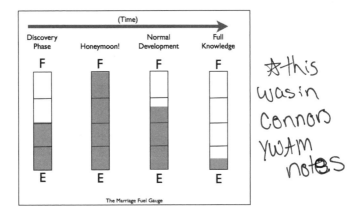

The Marriage Fuel Gauge

As you can see in my illustration, the first gauge in the discovery phase is already halfway full. That demonstrates the point in time when you both realize you are in love. It doesn't take long, once there has been mutual disclosure and acceptance of the feelings you have for each other, for the fuel gauge to start filling up. It's natural.

WARNING!

Hopefully *before* you get to the point of allowing yourself to fall in love with someone, the person has successfully passed your more important checklist, which includes answers to questions like:

1. What do, or would, my parents/family think about this person?

2. What about their character? (For example, what kinds of choices do they make when they think nobody is looking?)

3. What kind of family upbringing are they from? Am I ready to join my life and family with someone with this kind of background?

4. How does this person respond under pressure?

These are the kinds of questions that people used to entertain during courtship *prior* to making any major commitments of engagement or marriage. Young pairs were simply getting to know each other and their families to see if the match might be a right fit. Many people find themselves in divorce court these days because they did not consider these kinds of important questions prior to allowing themselves to fall in love with someone. It is possible to be "too in love for reason." Once the goo factor has kicked in, it is like trying to stop a train moving downhill.

Assuming that things are "all systems go" and you two are comfortable with the idea of pursuing engagement and marriage, you are well into the discovery phase. This time can be described with wonderful words like mystery, excitement, newness, hope, intrigue, and adventure. However, a critical thing to realize about this phase is that all of these things are automatic at this stage. It doesn't take much effort to fall in love. The newness, mystery, and sense of hope for the future is just there because you are getting to know this person. It is very easy to mistake goo for full knowledge.

What do I mean by "full knowledge"? In the discovery phase, we feel like we know the person intimately because we know their likes and dislikes. In many cases, we feel like we know each other so well that we can finish each other's sentences. Full knowledge is the point where we are intimately familiar with everything about the person that we would like to see change.

Ah, I can almost hear a young reader thinking to herself, "I don't want to change him. I love him just the way he is." Believe me. In time, your short list of attitudes, habits, and other things that rub you the wrong way about your life mate will grow. If your marriage partner is a human being, your list will grow. If you both plan to live in the same house together, your list will grow. If you intend to stay married for more than three days, your list will grow. If you think you might eat more than one meal a week together, your list will grow. If you think you might want to live a normal life together, your list will grow. And that brings us to the next stage on the fuel gauge after the wedding and honeymoon: *normal development.*

Normal Development

Notice how I skipped over the wedding/honeymoon section, which is how we all want our marriages to be, no matter how long we have been married. There is not much that needs to be said about "Full." When the love tank is full, everybody is happy, and when it's full, you know it. As I pointed out in the discovery phase above, this stage of the relationship is autopilot. If you get married on a tank that isn't full, you are probably making a fatal mistake. However, if you married on a partially full tank and it has never been filled up since, I am not suggesting that you try to get out now, but if the mutual fuel tank has never been full, this is an opportunity for your Christian faith to kick in. Pray for the Lord to begin working a two-fish, five-loaves kind of miracle in your situation. After all, He created you and your partner!

The line between the normal development and full knowledge phases is quite blurry, but let's look at some of the characteristics of both phases:

Normal Development	Full Knowledge (True Intimacy)
Reality	Faults
Boredom	Weaknesses
Familiarity	Character Flaws
Routine	(The Unexpected)
Temptation	

No matter how fabulous the honeymoon was or how thrilling the sex—given enough time, each marriage relationship will have the opportunity to experience at least one of the challenges mentioned above. It will not mean there is anything wrong with you or your spouse. If you notice, neither of the terms above could be categorized as sin. It's just a normal part of normal human beings trying to live a normal life together. The question is, how will you respond when you notice the fuel level has gone down some? You will have two choices, and you can decide right now, today, while reading this book, what your response is going to be. You can decide now that if you face these kinds of challenges, you will throw away the car because you couldn't be bothered to look for a gas station. Or you can plan to make some effort to refuel.

FULL KNOWLEDGE

At this point in the relationship, unpleasant traits about your mate are not only noticeable, they seem like they are going to be there forever. In most cases they have been there all along. You just never allowed yourself the luxury of making a point about it. Now it is starting to get old. The following words describe the kinds of things I'm talking about: *Faults. Weaknesses. Character Flaws.*

WARNING! SPECIAL ADVICE! TIP! KEY TO SUCCESS IN MARRIAGE!

Look for these things *before, before, before* allowing yourself to fall in love with a person. The Lord will graciously point them out to you if you are sincerely open to His leading. Again, realize that you are dealing with a human being, and, as my wife says, you are not marrying Jesus. Everyone has weaknesses. The question you have to ask yourself is, are you willing to live with this person's weaknesses for life, even if they never change? If your answer to that question is *yes,* and your potential partner's answer for themselves regarding your faults and flaws is *yes,* you might just be ready to move to the next level.

Nevertheless, you're married now (hypothetically speaking, since this book is only designed for people who have never been married before). You have two ways to react. One way is wrong (sin), and the other is righteous:

- Normal Development—WRONG
  REACTIONS (Sin)
  Reality: renege on vows
  Boredom: solitary entertainment
  Familiarity: verbal/physical abuse
  Routine: abandon structure
  Temptation: flirting/adultery

- Full Knowledge—WRONG REACTIONS (Sin)
  Faults: condescending verbal reminders/nagging
  Weaknesses: comparison with others
  Character flaws: passing judgment

Similar to shopping for any other big-ticket item, some people face a certain amount of "buyer's remorse" after marriage. There was a recent extreme case in the news of a young man who, the day after his wedding night, jumped off the top of a building in North Carolina and committed suicide. Although most people do not take that drastic of a step to deal with the reality of the commitment they have made, there are many cases of people reneging on their vows shortly after saying "I do." Reality hitting us in the face is normal. Expect it. Invite the Spirit of God to come in and help you through the season, and He will.

I am going to lump boredom, familiarity, and routine together. Routine can breed boredom. Some people respond by isolating themselves. No longer talking with their partner about their concerns or feelings because they supposedly already know what they're going to say, so what is the use in trying to communicate and discuss anything? Then things get so bad that if there is any verbal discussion, it ends up quickly becoming abusive, and may even become physical. It does not take long for this environment to snowball into a kind of hypersensitivity to your partner's faults, weaknesses, and character flaws. Reacting the wrong way to these can really get a relationship in trouble. In fuel-gauge terms, the relationship is probably running on fumes.

How does a relationship that started out with such a full tank get this low on fuel? Well, if you remember how the tank got full in the first place, it was *automatic*. It doesn't take much effort at first. I haven't bought very many brand-new cars, but when I have, one thing that was always certain: The new car already came with a full tank of fuel! It's automatic!

By the time you are in the normal development and full knowledge phases of a relationship, you need to do some things to refill the tank. Some relationships need refueling more frequently than others, but if there is any hope of your relationship not just coasting but zooming past the finished line, there are some practical things you can do to refuel. You have to take action.

+ Frequent forgiveness
+ Personal integrity check
+ Speedy repentance
+ Daily prayer (personal and together)
+ You initiate discussion

Frequent forgiveness

Jesus was asked how many times was enough to express forgiveness. His answer was seventy times seven. Now, because our postmodern society always has to challenge every absolute statement with extreme "well-what-about-this?" kinds of questions, please understand that I am not talking about a scenario where your marriage partner is sleeping around town, committing adultery on you night after night, that you need to stay married to them. I am talking about the daily infractions that we can allow to grow into lifelong emotional cancers.

Maria and I love each other more today than we ever have, but every day, without fail, one of us says or does something that hurts the other. Sometimes the infraction is so minor that forgiveness isn't even necessary to verbalize. We just do it and move on. Other times, a serious heart-to-heart talk is required. The key is to have that talk sooner rather than later. There is hardly anything better for getting the fuel tank refilled than a hefty dose of forgiveness asked for and forgiveness given. Very true!

Personal integrity check

The longer you are married, the more frequently you should review your side of the marriage vows. Plan to remind yourself, every now and then, of the promises you made on that day. Hopefully your partner will be willing to do the same thing. I recommend planning to do so at least on every anniversary. With today's technology, video images can affordably be stored and easily accessed for years to come. Plan to sit down and view the wedding video together at least once a year. Commit to and discuss refueling the tank.

Speedy repentance

News flash: human beings sin. The idea here is not for you to quickly point out your spouse's sin but your own. The Book of James says, "Confess your faults, one to another, and pray for one another that ye may be healed" (5:16, KJV).

I find that it is important to make a habit of confessing my sins to my wife and not just to Jesus alone. It's not easy. However, it actually serves as both a safeguard and deterrent from sin because I don't enjoy the experience.

Daily prayer

Here is one of the kingdom of God's best-kept secrets. One of the most intimate things you can do with your marriage partner is pray together.

About five years ago, Maria and I decided that we would start each new week off by spending an unrestricted time of prayer together on Monday mornings. We didn't realize when we started that God would use this regular commitment to pray together as a means of refilling our love tank. One of the main things this prayer time does is it gives us an opportunity to cleanse our hearts before God and ask forgiveness of each other if there is any little fracture someplace in our relationship.

The psalmist says, "If I regard iniquity in my heart, the Lord cannot hear me" (Ps. 66:18, KJV). In 1 Peter 3:7, Peter gives husbands instructions on how to treat their wives so that "[their] prayers will not be hindered."

Naturally, we pray together at times other than Monday mornings, but we treat that weekly appointment with the same level of importance as any scheduled business meeting, for example. Imagine a CEO of a major corporation trying to maintain a sense of focus and mission without ever meeting with others.

You initiate discussion

In most cases it is not the woman who needs to be encouraged to initiate discussion but the man. A recent scientific study concluded that over the course of a normal day, the average man speaks about one-third fewer words than the average woman. There is a phrase in Scripture that, in context, speaks to the people of God, challenging them to reevaluate their current perspective on things. The Lord demonstrates how to initiate interaction when He says, "Come now, let us reason together" (Isa. 1:18, KJV).

If there is a problem, no matter how tiny, don't let it go nor allow it to fester for days and days. You initiate some dialogue together. One of the Scriptures that has served our marriage well over the years is the one that admonishes, "Do not let the sun go down upon your wrath" (Eph. 4:26, KJV). *Important to me!*

Sometimes that requires a late-night conversation. It may even take some tears and time in order to reach a point of resolve.

Here is a tip. If there is a difficult matter than needs to be discussed and you anticipate the subject and details might be difficult for your spouse to handle, spend time praying for God to prepare them well before you bring the matter up. Sometimes one partner wants to launch into deep, volatile issues without any spiritual preparation. The Devil loves entering into unprepared places with his poison. Initiating a serious discussion without prayer preparation (and sometimes even fasting) can have as damaging results. A doctor would never walk into surgery right off the street without scrubbing down and wearing the proper clothing and equipment. *Need to do more often*

Human relationships are dynamic, and most people resist mechanical, technical approaches to relationship issues.

Nevertheless, there is one phrase that I recommend making part of your discussion-initiation language. Maria and I were introduced to this in our premarital counseling years ago, and it has served us well. No matter how confident you are that you are right and your spouse is wrong, respect them enough to give them the benefit of the doubt by starting your discussion something like this:

"I might be wrong, but the other day when you called me 'lazy' in front of the kids, that really hurt. Could we talk about what you meant?"

The challenge is to bring yourself to the point where you are not just saying the words because it's a formula you read in a book, but you really mean, "I might be wrong..." There have been times when I was absolutely confident that Maria said something barbed to me because she was trying to manipulate me into a certain action, only to discover, after much discussion and openness, that I had misunderstood her motive.

Sometimes one of us lets the flesh get into the equation. We occasionally get a good sarcastic jab in just to make our point. As the recipient of such a jab, Christ's way is not to jab back. Proverbs says, "A soft answer turns away wrath" (Prov. 15:1, NKJV).

Frequent forgiveness, personal integrity check, speedy repentance, daily prayer (personal and together), and initiate discussion. These are the essential "fuel" that your marriage will need regularly. There are also some "fuel treatment" systems out there that really help to add some extra punch to the fuel efficiency! Simple gifts and surprises that say "I love you" that are not attached to birthdays and anniversaries go a long way. No matter how busy you both are, schedule getaway times away from the demands of life, if only for a day or two. In other words, the same things that were automatic during the discovery phase should be revived in a fresh way, if you don't want your tank to run dry.

8

No Secrets in Marriage

ALTHOUGH IT IS not my intention to motivate readers with fear, I hope that this chapter will serve single Christians by inspiring them to take a sober look at the kinds of relationship traps many people find themselves in. Imagine falling in love with someone and marrying them, only to find out that they are entangled in a debilitating addiction or have trouble with the law and they managed to conceal it from you. Unfortunately, it happens every day.

The way I see it, there are at least two kinds of secrets. One is the kind of secret that is kept for the benefit of others, like a surprise birthday party. That kind of secret normally poses no intentional risk of danger, threat, or loss to anyone. The other kind of secret is designed to conceal sin or even crimes. Hiding money gained from the illegal sale of drugs, for instance, would be the wrong kind of secret to keep.

Many marriages today have a ticking time bomb in the very center of their relationship because somebody is maintaining a deep, dark secret. In some highly dysfunctional unions, partners are keeping terrible secrets from one another, and they intend to carry those secrets to their graves. The longer a bad secret goes before it is exposed, the more devastating the impact will be when the facts do come to light. The Bible indicates that on the day of judgment, all secrets will be revealed. It is much better to expose them and deal with them in the here and now than to keep up appearances.

Marriages are only as strong as the amount of trust the married partners have between them. On the surface, a couple can look like they have it all together. They can appear to be a loving, handholding, Romeo-and-Juliet, perfect specimen of wedded bliss, but if one or both of them are keeping a dark secret from the other, the core of their union is rotten. It is only a matter of time before the cancer will kill such a relationship.

A few years ago, there was the story in the news of a businessman who died of heart failure. As his estate was being sorted out, it came to light that the man had been maintaining a charade of being the faithful family man, only with two different family units in two different parts of the country! He would tell one wife and family that he had to fly out of town on business for a few days so he could go and check in with his other wife and family for a while. Eventually, he would have to tell that family the same lie so that he could fly back to spend time with the other family.

I realize this is a rare, unusual situation, but how did this man's problem advance to such a extreme level of deception? It probably started with maintaining one small secret of the wrong kind. In order to keep that secret viable, other lies had to be wedged underneath in order to prop it up. Without exposure of the secret and a willingness to repent, correcting it becomes not only difficult, but almost impossible to contemplate.

In this man's case, the truth did not come out until he was dead, but when it came out, the scars that the revelation left on the souls of his wives and children were absolutely cataclysmic. Everyone felt betrayed.

The Bible says, "Let your 'Yes' be 'Yes,' and your 'No' be 'No'" (Matt. 5:37). God's original design is that parents are supposed to be honest and do the right thing, then teach their children to be honest, do the right thing, and not lie. Then, as those children become adults, they are to model for their children the same principles, and so on. A society made up of family units committed to this simple system should result in lower crime rates, lower divorce rates, and a much more pleasant place to live. Obviously, that is not a picture that reflects our world today. Trust in the Lord's ability to guide you to the right mate. He knows all secrets.

How did I become such an expert in this subject? It was not through reading books or attending classes. It was largely through observation, but mostly through personal experience.

It would be easy for me to tell you story after story of people I have observed maintaining marriage-threatening secrets from their spouses, but I have come to realize that God wants to use my personal story of the road from bondage to freedom to help others become free. It is with my wife's permission and blessing that I include this very personal aspect of my story.

When I was a child, both of my parents worked to keep our family afloat. Every day, I was taken to a babysitter until Mom and Dad came to pick me up after work. The babysitter was a retired lady who had a preteen granddaughter that she was raising on her own. Although I was only four or five years old, this granddaughter introduced me to things that no five-year-old should know about. Nevertheless, this early education laid the groundwork for what would snowball into a lifestyle of secrecy and addiction.

Neither of my parents were committed believers in Christ at the time, so they allowed many aspects of the world to enter our lives and our home. At one point, around age nine, I remember the back seat of our car being full of pornographic magazines that I had to sit on. I don't recall my folks giving me any specific instructions not to look at them or flip through them, although in my heart I realized I shouldn't, so I didn't. But in most cases, there was enough titillating information on the covers alone to ignite intrigue in a young boy's mind.

By my early teenage years I started to find this material hidden (poorly) in my parents' bedroom, and I found opportunities to sneak in there and expose myself to the so-called adult entertainment, day after day, all without their knowledge.

Right up to the point that I became a Christian, by age seventeen a serious addiction had formed. In those days, because of the social stigma, access to pornography was not easy. Getting hold of it required a willingness to risk getting caught.

From those years to the time I got married at age twenty-five, my circumstances made it nearly impossible to even secretly gain access and exposure to porn. Although my incidents of consumption were no longer there, the stronghold remained dormant, but not dead, in my soul. I had come to accept the notion that I would never be free from the pattern of temptation, falling, guilt, repentance, forgiveness, and back to temptation again. I felt like the perfect example of the apostle Paul's description of the Christian struggle with sin in Romans 7:21–24:

> So I find this law at work: When I want to do good, evil is right there with me. For in my inner being I delight in God's law; but I see another law at work in the members of my body, waging war against the law of my mind and making me a prisoner of the law of sin at work within my members. What a wretched man I am! Who will rescue me from this body of death?

In the early days of my marriage, I only casually mentioned to my wife that I had prior struggles with this temptation. I didn't want to make a big deal about it because I had rationalized that since I was forgiven, there was no reason to dig up the past. Then along came the Internet and free access to millions of images and content, accessible in absolute secrecy. No one would ever know.

Over the years, I had shared my problem with various men of God, and their prayers for freedom sustained me, but I continually fell. It was not until God Almighty moved in a way that only He can that I was truly released from the power of this lifelong pattern of addiction. As I share my story of deliverance with others, I am often asked for specifics of how the Lord freed me. For me, it was one day that I read an article in *National Geographic* magazine that had absolutely nothing to do with pornography. In fact, the subject was more about my vocation than anything else, but God used it to do a deep work in my soul. I was very careful about proclaiming my freedom until sufficient time had passed so that I could see if it really stuck.

Remember a few paragraphs ago when I said that the longer a bad kind of secret is concealed before it is exposed, the more damaging the impact when it actually does come to light? Well, it was time to put the details of my struggle in the light with my wife. I sat her down and explained that for years I had struggled with this problem, even during our marriage, but now the Lord had truly set me free. Initially, she was crushed. She wept and wept for many reasons, as one might imagine. To add salt to the wound, she reminds me that it was our anniversary the day I broke the truth to her. Definitely not the best timing.

Being the woman of compassion she is, she graciously found it in her heart to forgive me and embrace my new freedom because of her commitment to our marriage. Remember "the third entity" in chapter 5?

Today, the power of God has renewed and strengthened our bond like never before. Maria is free to ask me at any time if I am in any way struggling with the old temptation. By His awesome grace and power, I am thrilled every time to honestly tell her that my freedom is complete and thorough.

My freedom is real, and any kind of draw toward my former lifestyle of secrecy is ineffective. However, at my initiation, and for my wife's own sense of continued confidence and trust in me, I make certain that she knows all of my Internet passwords. She has full access, and always will, to everything about me.

Many years ago, I heard relationship expert Dean Sherman say, "There are no guarantees in relationships." That phrase has always proven to be true in all the relationships I have observed between men and women. It is always possible that even though both parties agree to disclose various things to one another, invariably some secret can surface and cause great pain to both. You really only have control over your own behavior and choices.

What are some ways to safeguard your marriage before it even starts from the devastating effects of the wrong kinds of secrets? Here are a few:

1. Determine before God to actively seek help and advice with regard to any kind of issue that entangles you, i.e., gambling, debt, alcohol, drugs, whatever. Depending on the severity, it may cost you seriously, like it did the young man who saw the film *The Passion of the Christ*. After being moved by the film's content, he decided to confess to having murdered his girlfriend. Hopefully your secret is not as drastic as that, but better to deal with it now than later.

2. Promise yourself and God that you will not allow yourself to develop an intimate relationship with someone until you know that you are willing to share with them anything and everything necessary. If you are currently involved (engaged,

courting, etc.), ask the Lord to help you and your dear one to develop an environment of open sharing and trust together.

3. Because of the way technology has evolved, the Internet has made it possible for people to develop inappropriate relationships without ever meeting face to face. Secret Internet accounts, for example, can be established and accessed without anyone close to you ever knowing.

   Here is a rule of thumb that should be the guide of every Christian: just because you *can* doesn't mean you *should*. Just because you *can* make use of free Internet access at the public library doesn't mean you should. Just because you *can* visit the boy's dorm at night doesn't mean you should. Just because you *can* spend your money on lottery tickets without your partner knowing about it doesn't mean you should. Just because you *can* go to that industry conference alone with that attractive co-worker, even though you are both staying in separate rooms, doesn't mean you should go to that industry conference.

4. Identify all possible situations that might allow you an opportunity to be tempted to develop a secret of the wrong kind. Expose that opportunity to someone you love and trust, and invite them to hold you accountable in some way.

The other day I dropped my kids off for an hour-long play practice. I realized that I had an hour of free time on my hands, so I decided to go to the software store and look at some software I had been thinking about purchasing. The store is all the way on the other side of town. On my way there, I realized that I had not mentioned to Maria that I had any intention of going to that store. Even though I had absolute freedom to go to the software store, on my way there I decided to simply phone my wife and let her know that I was going to go across town. Why? What difference would it make if she knew I was going there or not? We have developed the practice of making sure we know each other's approximate whereabouts and activities at all times, for many reasons. Some of it has to do with safety and potential emergencies. It is our way of fortifying a sense of trust in one another.

Don't let secrets spoil your marriage. Determine before you even get married that you are going to enter this exciting adventure free and clear of any of the Devil's encumbrances. Cultivate the habit of walking in the light.

"But if we walk in the light as He is in the light, we have fellowship with one another, and the blood of Jesus Christ His Son cleanses us from all sin" (1 John 1:7, NKJV).

9

Careers and Marriage

I HOPE THAT BY this point you are developing an increased respect for the value of marriage. If I haven't stressed it enough, here it comes again. Be careful about who you allow yourself to fall in love with. Once your emotions are in gear, you might as well be trying to stop a moving train headed downhill.

This chapter highlights a few scenarios that get down to the nitty-gritty of functioning day in and day out with your marriage partner. Since most people are not independently wealthy nor living on an overstuffed trust fund, the average adult spends about one-third of his day earning a living. That leaves another third for sleep, and the remaining third of each twenty-four-hour period is usually spent either in a part-time job or spending time with family, hobbies, watching TV, or outdoor activities.

Some marriages suffer and fail because of an imbalance and conflict over how each partner spends his or her day. The Bible warns, "Do not be unequally yoked together with unbelievers" (2 Cor. 6:14, NKJV).

The reasoning behind that is simple. If you believe that Jesus Christ of Nazareth is the risen Son of God who died for the sins of all mankind and is coming again someday to receive all the redeemed into His eternal kingdom, and your spouse is an atheist, someone is going to have to do some major compromising if you are going to live in peace together.

Before I explain why I think we can apply the above passage of Scripture to other contexts of life, let's examine the simple agricultural analogy of a yoke and its purpose. In many parts of the world today, farmers still rely on beasts of burden for hauling, plowing, and such. In much of Asia, where I spent several years as a missionary, some oxen actually have a natural hump on the back of their neck, which provides the perfect place to hook up various wooden farm equipment that the animal pulls behind them. Although many farmers can function just fine with one ox, if two oxen are connected together by a yoke, their combined power makes work more efficient. Here's why:

+ Each animal is only bearing half the total weight of whatever it is they are pulling together.

+ This distributed load allows each animal to maintain their stamina, making it possible for each to work longer than one animal doing the same amount of work alone could do.

In order for this system to work, both animals have to be similar in kind, weight, height, health, and so on. For example, most farmers would not attempt to yoke a mule and a cow together. The results could be quite comical. But worse than that, imagine having one ox facing north, yoked to another ox facing south. I don't think very much valuable work would get done. In fact, the farmer's best chance of getting anything profitable out of this arrangement might be to sell tickets to the spectacle!

The amazing thing is, thousands of married couples try to function unequally yoked every day, with no end in sight. Their ultimate task together is to cultivate a thriving, healthy marriage and legacy, but one partner's career life has them facing north and the other is facing south.

Here are just a few examples of the many marriage/career scenarios that I have seen. I recommend you try to avoid the weaker examples and emulate the stronger ones. The names and exact circumstances have been changed so that my dear friends won't get angry with me for using them as examples!

Trevor and Wendy

Trevor and Wendy have been married for almost ten years now. They don't have any children, and because they married relatively late in life, starting a family (including children) does not seem to be likely. The community that they live in is high intensity, and densely populated, so sometimes just finding a parking spot outside their apartment can cause their stress level to reach the boiling point. The cost of living in their community is so high that they have to hang on tight to their jobs, even if there is little opportunity for advancement. Obligations to one of their senior family members also forces them to remain in this stressful environment indefinitely.

Trevor and Wendy kiss each other goodbye in the morning and then head off to different parts of the city to spend the bulk of their day at their respective jobs. It is almost impossible for them to ever consider getting together for lunch because of travel distance. By the time they get back together again in the evening, they are both exhausted and can hardly wait to go to bed and rest up for the next day's grueling schedule.

The good news is, Trevor and Wendy both are committed Christians and appear to have every intention of remaining true to their promise to each other. They manage to cope by scheduling quiet getaways together, sometimes to other countries. Trevor is in a career transition, but they are being careful not to make any drastic changes so they don't disrupt their finances completely. Although their situation is intense, Trevor and Wendy seem to be making it all work.

Lance and Yvonne

Lance and Yvonne didn't make it, though. What happened? They are also Christians. They fell head-over-heels in love. Lance is a professional recording artist. Yvonne is a professional dancer in a major ballet company. On the surface, that looks like it would work out to be the perfect match—two artists who love God and love each other.

Like our two oxen yoked together but facing different directions, so were Lance and Yvonne. His tour itinerary had him on the road about two hundred days out of the year. The record company could care less about Lance's marriage. He needed to be out there promoting albums that they had invested thousands of dollars in.

Yvonne's dance career had been her whole reason for living, up to the point that she and Lance met. There was no way she was going to sacrifice the career she had trained for all her life in order to traipse around the globe listening to Lance sing. Two years into the marriage, they were divorced. Had they individually sought good counsel prior to falling in love and making a marriage commitment, they would probably have decided against marrying if neither was able or willing to make major adjustments to their careers. In order for there to be such thing as quality time together, there has to be some level of quantity time together.

Mindy and Max

Mindy and Max have been married for about sixteen years. They met one another while working for the same organization. Although they grew up in completely different countries, their passions and career callings are exactly the same. Their personalities and temperaments are also similar.

Because they work for the same company, Mindy and Max are privileged to travel together frequently. They spend their working hours together, they sleep together, and they spend their leisure time together. As funny as it may sound to some, they often wear matching clothes! I can't think of another couple that is more equally yoked than Mindy and Max.

Does that mean that you have to be each other's clone in order for your marriage to succeed? Of course not. But if you had to choose which situation you would rather find yourself in, I think Mindy and Max have the best chance of ending each day with a smile on their faces.

A serious question that I challenge you to face is this: which is more important to you, your career or your marriage? What if you work midnight to 9 a.m. while your spouse is a regular 9-to-5 employee? If neither of you is willing to look for something that would allow you to spend more quality time together, your job is more valuable to you than your marriage.

To the person who earns tons of money working for a company that has them flying around the world three weeks out of every month, I would recommend to anyone to think twice before marrying. As best as humanly possible, find out what his or her future plans and goals are. Find out if they would be willing to take an alternative schedule that would allow for more time together with the family.

As of this writing, there is no talk, politically, in the US about reinstating the draft. Consequently, everyone in the US military is there because they choose to be there. The government determines where you will live and when you will go there. Sometimes deployments last from six months to two years at a time. These are very serious considerations for people contemplating marriage. Military marriages have made it before, but many struggle with the challenges of temptation, adultery, extreme loneliness, and so forth. Don't leap into a situation like this without counting the cost.

A final thought. Very few people in Western society spend a lifetime working for the same company, even if they do have some sense of longevity with a company. Naturally, then, it is impossible to make the perfect decision about whom to marry based on their present situation alone. As years go by, people often make career moves. Sometimes they decide to pursue an advanced degree. This kind of unforeseen decision often puts huge stress on families and marriages. Some make it through the maze unharmed. Many do not. Do yourself the favor of at least considering both of your career dispositions before making the ultimate commitment.

10

Money and Marriage

RESEARCH TELLS US that money and disagreements about what to do with it is the number-one trigger for divorce. One person works hard to earn money, for example, and in a matter of moments, the other one spends it frivolously. Or maybe one person thinks it is perfectly fine to deplete the savings account in order to care for an ailing parent, but their spouse would rather find another means of financing the loved one's senior years. One parent might be convinced that private, Christian school is the absolute only option for their children's education, but the other spouse wonders why it is so necessary to "spend all that money" on private education when public schools are able to offer a rigorous education on the government's dime.

The first thing I want to recommend is that you develop a basic, biblical philosophy about money while you are single and unattached. Test your approach to money against the Scriptures. Give yourself the opportunity to experience the living God's involvement in your finances before joining your finances permanently with someone else's.

Many people enter the work force in their late teens and early twenties. In most cases they are still living with their parents or guardians. In that situation, there are some built-in support systems that do not allow the young adult to feel the full weight of financial responsibility. It's not about how much money you have, but rather about what you do with the money you earn.

Just today, prior to starting to work on this chapter, I was talking with some friends from church. A mother of three young men confided in us that she was having trouble figuring out what her youngest son was doing with the money he earns from his job. He does not attend school (college) and still lives at home with Mom and Dad. He has never opened a bank account of any kind, yet he remains up-to-date with the latest fashions.

This Christian young man is unaware of the negative fruit that his financial shortsightedness might bear in his life. Unless he makes some major changes in how he handles money, his bad habits will not automatically change when he gets married. In fact, they will probably end up becoming a major source of friction in his marriage.

Money problems may be the number-one cause of marriage problems, but what is the number-one cause of money problems? I propose that the main cause of money problems is financial immaturity. Just because a person has all the physical features of a mature adult does not mean that they are indeed mature. The good news is, it does not require an MBA degree in business or finances to be financially mature. All it takes is a basic, biblical philosophy of money and the discipline to live by that philosophy.

I have discovered that of all the good things the Bible describes about how to use money, there are five basic ways to maximize it. These five things are most effective if learned and practiced early in life. They are:

- Tithing – need to practice this more
- Savings
- Giving

+ Living

+ Investing

I call this the "power budget" because I find that believers who practice these things will find that their faith unlocks biblical promises of multiplied resources.

Tithing

The Bible calls tithing the first fruits of all your labor. Ten percent of our income, according to the Scriptures, belongs to God. Even though we work for it and it is part of our paycheck, it does not belong to us.

Before any other financial obligations are addressed, we are obligated to God. Malachi 3:8–12 reads:

> "Will a mere mortal rob God? Yet you rob me.
>
> "But you ask, 'How are we robbing you?'
>
> "In tithes and offerings. You are under a curse—your whole nation—because you are robbing me. Bring the whole tithe into the storehouse, that there may be food in my house. Test me in this," says the LORD Almighty, "and see if I will not throw open the floodgates of heaven and pour out so much blessing that there will not be room enough to store it. I will prevent pests from devouring your crops, and the vines in your fields will not drop their fruit before it is ripe," says the LORD Almighty. "Then all the nations will call you blessed, for yours will be a delightful land," says the LORD Almighty."

The practice of tithing distinguishes God's people from everybody else. Logically, tithing does not make sense. Why would someone on a modest income "give away money" (to God somehow) before addressing their other obligations and desires?

It takes faith to be a tither. It requires a basic faith that God exists. It takes faith to believe that the Bible is true and has relevance to our lives. It requires faith to expect that what the above Scripture says is going to happen is really going to happen.

I meet every so often with a buddy from church. He is climbing back from having made some mistakes in several areas of his life. When we began talking about tithing, he mentioned that he has never seen it as a logical thing to do because the 10 percent "missing" from his income would cause him to come up short on his monthly bills. He went on to say that what he does have coming in is not even enough. My response to him was, "That's where faith comes in." Two fish and five loaves of bread is not enough to feed five thousand people. But when it was given to the Lord, unusual things began to happen, according to the Scripture.

Maria and I have faithfully practiced tithing for our entire married life. Numerous times we were bone dry financially, but God has come through with inexplicable, abundant blessings from seemingly nowhere time and time again.

I was hired to direct a docudrama recently. I did my job to the best of my ability, and the client paid me promptly. We were all settled, as far as the contract is concerned. Several months later, I was invited by the client to discuss the possibility of doing another project together. As I left the meeting, the client slipped me an envelope with a thank you note inside, along with a bonus check for $5,000—no strings attached! Talk about floodgates of blessing!

Although I could spend a few chapters sharing examples of God fulfilling His promises regarding tithing, suffice it to say, I highly recommend it as a serious starting point for anyone whose finances seem to be coming up short. Develop your own track record of God's faithfulness through tithing before you get married. Then be on the lookout for a potential life partner who has their own history of experiencing God's faithfulness to them as a result of a lifestyle of tithing. When two lives like that come together—watch out, world!

Saving

God only asks for 10 percent. This means He is leaving it up to us to figure out what we will do with the remaining 90 percent. I do not claim to be a financial expert. However, if a person (especially one living on a fixed income) makes it a practice to consume the whole of their remaining 90 percent, no matter how small or large it is, that person will hardly ever have enough money, even though they tithe. Ask me how I know.

The purpose of savings is to increase financial stability. (Remember, the number-one cause of divorce is money problems.)

Because my parents were not mentored in this stuff, they were not equipped to be able to model it to me. As a kid, I once asked my dear mother, "Mom, why do people save money?" Unfortunately, she did not have a good answer because she was not in the practice of doing it herself. She and Dad were in the trap of consuming most of what came in because that's all they knew to do at the time. (If you are reading this book, you do not have that excuse.) Mom and Dad became believers in Christ later in my life, so we have grown together over the years in this area.

The Book of Proverbs advises, "He that gather's money little by little makes it grow" (Prov. 13:11).

What is the purpose of "growing" money? News alert: money is actually good stuff! Yes, the Bible says "the *love* of money is the root of all kinds of evil," but actually having some is more beneficial than having none.

In order for you and your future spouse to grow money, however, you have to be of a mind-set that a portion of your money is never available to be consumed. Your savings should be one of the safest, stable aspects of your portfolio not ever to be consumed, not even by emergencies! When something is consumed, it is no longer available.

Savings should work like a fruit tree. The tree itself represents your savings fund. I am not saying your savings needs to be a bank account necessarily. There are many instruments to use for saving. The savings fund produces fruit. Harvest the fruit from the tree and take it to market (invest). Don't chop the whole tree down and eat all the fruit yourself. You will have nothing if you continually do that!

Here is my recommendation. Do not take it as legal or financial advice. Take it for what it is—advice from a guy writing a book on how to prepare for marriage: save early and often. Once your savings reaches a certain level that you predetermine, skim a portion of that money off and invest the funds into the safest, most valuable, tangible asset(s) you can;—real estate, for example. Then continue to save until it reaches a level where you can do the same kind of thing again and again and again. The next thing you know, you may even become financially independent!

Remember, you and your spouse are looking to launch a legacy. That means something that lasts beyond your own lifetime. Proverbs also says, "A good person leaves an inheritance to his children's children" (Prov. 13:22). That means grandchildren. You might be a twenty-two-year-old, reading this and thinking, *This guy is crazy. Why should I even need to be thinking about grandchildren already? I'm young. I've got my whole life ahead of me.* Yes, that is the normal, shortsighted perspective under which most of the world functions, but you are not like the world. You are operating from a platform of faith and the blessing of God in your life and an understanding that your life is not all about you.

Giving

Since your life is not all about you, a portion of every dollar you earn should also be allocated to giving. Just like you allocate a set percentage as your tithe, I recommend setting aside a percentage for giving.

The Bible says, "Whoever is kind to the poor lends to the Lord" (Prov. 19:17). This is yet another category where faith in God's Word makes it possible to experience His creative multiplying power in our material lives. Jesus says, "Give, and it shall be given unto you, pressed down, shaken together, and running over, will be put into your bosom" (Luke 6:38, NKJV).

Here comes a point that just might set some readers free from a sense of guilt when they are not able to respond to every request for money that comes their way. Setting aside a set percentage of your income for giving accomplishes two things:

+ It allows you to fulfill your biblical responsibility to be a cheerful giver.
+ It allows you to rest, free of condemnation, when you have to say no.

Certainly, it is all about attitude. Everyone I have ever heard of, myself included, who has ever felt led by God to give away everything they have, has subsequently seen God come through with meeting their own needs. The Bible only records one time where Jesus asked someone to give away absolutely everything they owned, and that was the rich, young ruler. As disciples of Christ, we always have to be mindful that everything we have is His anyway and should be joyfully relinquished if He asks us to. However, His request of the rich young ruler was a rare one.

Maria and I have found that since we decided that a set percentage of our income will be allocated to giving, there is a certain excitement in giving that we have not experienced before.

We also treat the giving category similar to the tithe, in that we don't miss the money because we consider it not ours anyway. We are just momentary caretakers of the funds. What is really fun, though, is seeing God multiply back to us in ways that only can be explained as His doing!

Living

When I first became a Christian at age seventeen, I met a bubbly, cowboy kind of character at a big evangelistic outreach event in Virginia. He and I worked together on the construction team building a large outdoor stage for the event. He realized I was a new believer, so he sort of took me under his wing for the few days we worked together. Of all the insights and stories he shared with me, I will never forget this one. With a huge cowboy grin on his face, he said, "Kenny, I have never felt closer to God than I do right now." When I asked him why, he told me that it was because he is now living on 10 percent of his income, and he gives God the remaining 90! It has taken me more than thirty years of living and walking with God to finally see the power in that man's lifestyle.

The world says the more you keep, the more you'll have. And the more you have, the better life is. Jesus says, "Whoever clings to his life will lose it, but he that loses his life for my sake and the gospel will find it" (Matt. 10:39).

My cowboy buddy had found a secret. Contentment. The Bible says, "Godliness with contentment is great gain" (1 Tim. 6:6). The more you give, the more that comes back your way. But if you are content with a certain amount of money to live on, you know that what comes your way above and beyond that might be for something other than consuming on yourself.

How does it work? Step one: decide on a "contentment goal." This concept was eye-opening to me. One day, recently, I felt the Lord ask me, "Kenny, how much money would you be *content* to live on?" I did not get the sense that this was a trick question in any way, so I came up with a dollar figure that even included a few non-necessities. Then I felt the Lord say (not audibly, but in that still, small voice the Bible describes), "Good—that figure is not your financial goal, but it represents 10 percent of your financial goal."

God has an interesting way of stretching our faith. In my case, He wisely had me first commit to a contentment figure. Then He challenged me to begin believing and praying for income that is ten times that amount! One of the things I have learned over the years, when it comes to figuring out what words are from God and which ones are not, is that God usually challenges me to believe for something that is impossible for me to accomplish without Him.

Am I living on 10 percent of my income right now? Well, I am working and praying toward that goal. So, we have tithed, saved some, and set aside a percentage for giving. Now, the living category covers needs and wants, like housing, transportation, food, entertainment, utilities, taxes, and insurance. Before we discuss the fifth category of investing, I want to talk about debt and emergency funds.

My church buddy, who I said has not been tithing until recently, raised the issue of debt when we were talking about God and financial matters one day. When I mentioned to him about this fivefold financial philosophy, he said the only reason he could not see not consuming the remaining 90 percent on his needs was because he was in significant debt.

In today's society, debt is easy to get into, and often very challenging to rise out of. According to recent statistics, the average American with credit cards carries more than $10,000 in balances year after year. By only paying the minimum balances over a long period of time, the consumer ends up paying significantly more to the creditor than the actual purchase was worth. Living like this can virtually cancel out the benefit and value of any savings and investments.

Find a way to work your way out of debt with a portion of your *living* money. It might take some sacrifices and even taking on some part-time employment to satisfy outstanding debt, but anyone serious about not dragging money problems into their marriage will recognize that uncontrolled debt is a major enemy.

Investing

I have known a little bit about investing for most of my adult life. Unfortunately, it has only been in recent years that Maria and I have taken concrete steps towards making the most of the little we've had. For some reason we thought we would invest when we could afford to. We were waiting for some major windfall to come our way and we would be able to invest. Being full-time volunteer missionaries for more than half our lives, we lived in the financial camp that says, "Hey, we didn't come here to stay. Heaven is our home, so let's do all our investing into the work of the Lord."

Even though God honors a healthy perspective of eternal value versus earthly value, we are supposed to make the most of what He gives us stewardship over on the earth. Jesus tells the story of a man who became irate with one of his servants who buried the man's money in the ground while the man had gone away, rather than investing it and earning some interest. This servant was considered foolish for wasting the opportunity he had to turn the little he was entrusted with into more. His contemporaries, on the other hand, were considered wise because they were able to demonstrate that they had generated money above what they started out with.

So, what is the purpose of investing? Do we multiply wealth so that there is money to buy bigger boats, take longer vacations, and drive fancier cars? Although there is nothing wrong with those things, we must remind ourselves of the contentment factor. If our investments yield significant profits, what do we do with the money?

I believe the purpose of investing is to gradually provide a platform from which to increase one's influence for the kingdom of God on the earth. The increase of one's "holdings" often results in a proportionate level of influence. This influence is not for the purpose of lording it over people, but rather to gain access into people's lives in order to make a deposit of the kingdom of God.

How much money should you invest? Take the same approach as we have looked at in the other four categories. Decide on a comfortable percentage of every dollar that you earn, and tuck it away for investment purposes. Do you know when the best time to start investing is? When you are still living with Mom and Dad! Why? Because, in most cases, they are taking care of the "living" category for you.

If only I had the chance to go back to the days when I was sixteen, working part-time at McDonalds, and bringing home about $300 every two weeks. My parents were taking care of every other aspect of my needs. It was the perfect situation for me to begin building some net worth. Unfortunately, I'll never see any of that money again. Guess where it all went. Most of it went to pay for long-distance phone calls to girls living in other parts of my state. If only I knew then what I know now.

The last point I want to make about marriage and money has to do with "the Big Day." The world is as full of different wedding traditions as it is of different peoples on the earth. One thing that is common, though, is the fact that weddings usually cost money. In some cases, a parent may take on the burden of the expenses of the wedding. In other cases, as it was with our wedding, Maria and I lived overseas, and neither of our parents had much money. Therefore, we had to take on the expenses involved with getting ourselves hitched.

Fortunately, I married a very levelheaded woman, and I would like to think she thinks as much about me! As it pertains to our wedding expenditures, Maria's feet were on the ground. Although she had great dreams of what her wedding day would be like, we were both in agreement that we would not put ourselves into debt so heavy that our early years of marriage would be stressed unnecessarily.

Agree!

The Scriptures promise that the man who finds a wife becomes eligible for favor from the Lord. I saw that principle start working immediately. Only God can make it possible for two non-salaried missionaries to enjoy a beautiful wedding in an Anglican church in Hong Kong, attended by a couple hundred people, then a fun and lively reception with a beautiful wedding cake made by a Swiss baker friend. We had just enough money to spend about three nights together in a nice hotel. The second day of our honeymoon, we received an unexpected gift package from a friend who wanted to send us to Thailand for a few days. We flew to Thailand and were met by some other missionary friends who decided to fly us to a beautiful resort area for a couple weeks! Our first days of marriage were so wonderful and memorable. The great thing is, we had zero debt to pay off afterwards. God blessed us with a dream wedding experience, all by trusting Him, step by step.

My point is, as you prepare for marriage, do your best to avoid creating financial problems for yourself right from the beginning. Start operating in these five areas now. Find a life partner whose perspective on money merges smoothly with yours, and then you can build toward a lifestyle of being a blessing, not only to each other, but also to those around you.

11

Preparing for Children

ONCE IN A while I ask my three children a series of questions. It is basically the same series of questions so that I can compare their current answers to previous answers that they have given me. The other day, I asked my youngest son the series:

Dad: Micah. Why are you going to school?

Micah: So I can learn.

Dad: Why do you need to learn?

Micah: So I can get good grades and go to a good university.

Dad: Why do you want to go to a good university?

Micah: So that I can get a good job.

Dad: Why do you want a good job?

Micah: So that I can be a good father and husband and provide for my family.

You may be surprised to learn that these values have not been forced on Micah. Maria and I have not brainwashed him so that whenever someone presses the right button, out comes a string of pat answers. He has come to these conclusions on his own, just from observation and hanging around. I am glad my son wants to be a good father and husband. It is an honor to think that I might be doing something that would cause him to esteem parenthood and marriage in that way.

The Bible says that children are a blessing from the Lord. When you are young and in "goo," however, the responsibility of twenty-four-hours a day, seven-days-a-week parenthood is not foremost on your list of motivations to get married. Some people marry without giving any serious thought to children. They figure it will work itself out when the time comes. After all, reproduction is a natural part of the process, right? Depending on your theology, that time could come sooner than you think.

I realize that there are at least two schools of thought among Christians on the subject of birth control. Some believe that birth control is against the will of God and that families should grow as large as the couple's reproductive years allow. Others feel that they are free, biblically and otherwise, to take any lawful and safe measures necessary, short of abortion, to control the number of children they bring into the world.

Either route you choose, it would be in your best interest to at least come to a personal conviction on the following three issues, with regard to children:

+ Your ideal family size
+ Education standards
+ Discipline methods and standards

FAMILY SIZE

A popular song from years ago says, "All We Need Is Love." The notion here is, "If we love each other, everything else will work itself out." Like anything of value in life, love will be tested. For some couples, it is tested when they come face to face with opposing views on whether or not to have kids in the first place.

One of the major keys to success in marriage is the elimination of surprise. Some readers would be shocked to learn how many people get married without ever discussing their individual perspective on children.

Consider this scenario. Evan meets Katie on a double date where their respective college roommates match them up. They are immediately attracted to each other on a physical level. They start hanging out together. Before long, they have crossed the "emotional point of no return." Neither Evan nor Katie have ever felt this way before. This is definitely love as far as they are concerned.

At this point in the relationship, it would be impossible for them to experience a breakup without someone being hurt deeply. Also, both parties are willing to make enormous concessions and compromises just to keep the relationship going.

They get married. Katie is ready to start having kids from day one. A family is what she has been dreaming of all her life. Evan is shocked when he finds out that she is not on the pill. Houston, we have a problem!

When would the better time for Evan and Katie to disclose their views on child bearing have been? Naturally, there is no exact right time that is right for every couple. In Evan and Katie's case, I would say that it is a topic worth casually introducing into their conversations prior to hitting the point of no return.

Once again, we need to go back to God's original design. God's original plan is that children grow up in a loving household with two parents who love one another. When those children become adults, they consult with their parents, whom they trust to advise them wisely about spouse selection and family life. Also, the children's own upbringing should have had such a positive impact on them that they want to emulate the environment they grew up in.

What does the Bible say about family size? The main Scripture that speaks to this says, "Happy is the man whose quiver is full of them [children]" (Ps. 127:5). How many is a full quiver? I dare say, as many as the Lord chooses to bless you with!

EDUCATION STANDARDS

In the US there are four choices, and the first one is illegal: no school, homeschool, private school, and public school. This decision can become another point of disagreement and strife between a couple, especially if they have not discussed it prior to marriage. But there may be other factors that can weigh in on the direction of your child's education, apart from your personal preferences.

All children are different. Each child is an individual. While one child may thrive in a homeschool environment, another needs frequent interaction with others and finds homeschooling depressing. I know some Christian parents who took their high-schoolers out of Christian school because the kids wanted to take on the challenge of being Christian witnesses among non-Christian kids.

Some families carry on long traditions of attending certain academic institutions, and to deviate from that tradition could introduce all sorts of other conflict. Imagine marrying someone and not knowing something so deep-seated and important to him or her.

Economics could be a major factor in education choice. I know of families that can barely keep themselves afloat financially, yet because of a fear that their children could be wrongly influenced in public school, they bend over backwards to keep them in Christian school, costing more money than they seem able to afford.

Our oldest son, David, spent his first two education years in Christian school. It was a wonderful, challenging environment for him. If we had it to do all over again, we would do it the same way. However, by the time he was ready for the next grade level, we could no longer afford to keep him there. Because of the requirements of my career path, I would not be able to be actively involved with home schooling David. With English being Maria's second language, she did not have the confidence to take on the responsibility of home schooling. That left us with no alternative but public school. Not only has it worked out to be the perfect solution for our family so far, but both of David's siblings after him have excelled in the public school system.

We found that success in the public school system required regular parental involvement with our children and the educators. If you feel that your child is being taught something that does not support a biblical worldview, that is where you jump in as a parent and dialogue with your child, and, if need be, with the school.

If your life's circumstances have you living in a dangerous neighborhood and your children would be in obvious danger in public school, it would be unwise to put them there anyway. We all have to learn to be led by the Spirit of the Lord in these and all other major decisions.

I have seen positive experiences in home school, Christian school, and public school. I also know of negative examples from each. For instance, just ten miles away from my previous home in Virginia Beach, a student in a prominent Christian school walked into the classroom and shot one of his teachers to death over a grade dispute. It is the only on-campus murder in our area on record to date, and it happened at a Christian school!

In another situation, a network of homeschool families agreed to bring their children together once each week for social and educational interaction. At one such gathering the police had to be called because one of the students brought a gun.

While I am encouraging you to plan ahead, prior to marriage, always remember that you have help. When the time comes to make educational decisions for your children, Proverbs 3:5–6 will work for you: "Trust in the Lord with all your heart." God loves our children even more than we possibly can. He always knows what is best for them.

DISCIPLINE METHODS AND STANDARDS

Here is a good topic of conversation for you and your potential marriage partner: to spank or not to spank? If so, what will you use? The hand? A rod or some other implement? If not, what will you do—just let them grow out of it? Will you remove privileges? What about "time outs"?

These are some of the questions that you and your legacy partner should have before you commit. The worst thing for your child would be for them to detect that you are not both on the same page with regard to their discipline. Try not to correct each other about discipline in front of your child. Their world is most stable when Mom and Dad are in agreement, even if they are in agreement against what the child wants.

The technical term for spanking is *corporal punishment*. Laws vary from state to state and country to country. What does the Bible say? Lots: "Train a child in the way he should go, and when he is old he will not depart from it" (Prov. 22:5–6).

It is not a matter of which method of discipline you *prefer*.

It is ultimately about what kind of legacy you want to leave. Psychology says our values are shaped in the first five years of our lives.

FAMILY TRADITIONS

In American society, *tradition* has become a negative word. Our society seems to be more interested in spontaneity and the unpredictable. These can also be good, but there is a positive aspect of tradition that needs to be celebrated by young families. Young children *love* tradition. They appreciate things they can count on being there on a regular basis.

Recently, Maria introduced a new tradition in our household. I don't think it will last long, but there have not been many objections so far. For our family, dessert is not daily, but when we have it, it's usually fruit. We eat far less sugar than most of the families we know. Nevertheless, from now until further notice, on Fridays dessert will be ice cream! Like I said, kids love tradition.

When my youngsters were quite small, I felt the Lord inspired me to introduce and establish a new family tradition. It was one that I had never heard of before. The goal and purpose of this tradition is to create a long-lasting, positive memory in each of my children's minds and lives. The memory of this tradition should be so impressive that my children would actually consider passing it on in their own families. We'll see. Our tradition? I mentioned it before in the chapter on keeping promises and vows. It is the "apprenticeship year."

In agricultural societies, children learn the ins and outs of farming from their fathers and mothers early in life. They learn how to operate farm equipment, attend to the needs of animals, and many other aspects of the farming life. Well, my children do not live on a farm, but the thought came to me that, without manipulating them to have to be what I am when they grow up, I could teach them important things that would be useful to them. Therefore, our family tradition is that when each child turns eight years old, they begin his or her apprenticeship year. That child gets to travel with me at least once during the year. The child also helps me with various tasks, such as booking airline tickets, writing checks, and lots more. The amazing thing is, prior to the eighth birthday, they could hardly wait until it was their turn. The child had something to look forward to with great anticipation. It was up to me to make it worth the wait.

Our family has maintained another very simple tradition that Maria and I both believe is an improvement to the way we grew up. We make it a point to eat our evening meal together without television. Because she is the best cook in the house, Maria does not just slap together something easy and fast. She usually prepares a meal that one would pay a good price for in the average restaurant. I make it a point to ask probing questions of the children about their day. When I get the sense that they are getting bored with that, we play some mental trivia games and brain teasers, inspired by the hit TV show, *Who Wants to Be a Millionaire?* "Is that your final answer?"

Our goal is to give our children such positive memories that they will make it a point to create similar family environments, perpetuating the legacy.

My final thought on preparing for children is possibly an unusual one. It has to do with communicating your values to posterity.

Some people's ancestors have somehow documented their perspectives on life. As someone serious about launching a legacy, you have to think this way.

A good friend recently asked me to help her produce a simple videotape. She came to my little studio, and I set her in front of a nice background. For about thirty minutes, she spoke directly to the camera and told each of her children how much she loves them and what her dreams for them are. I think there is value in taking it even a step further and giving a few words of timeless advice to those who are yet to be born. Imagine being able to see and hear, or at least read, something a forefather dictated to you before you were even born!

In another instance, the journalist in me began shouting that I should record a personal interview with Brother Andy, the senior-most member of my home church. Although he is in his eighties, Brother Andy is still with us, and I expect he will be for quite some time. Regardless, I convinced him to allow me to interview him on camera, where I asked him to tell me all about his life. His daughter later expressed her sincere appreciation for the video and that she even learned some things that she had not known before.

Even though you may not be at this stage of life yet, put this idea in your back pocket, and be thinking about ways you might strengthen your legacy by communicating with generations to come.

Now that You're Engaged, Why Wait for the Wedding Night?

YOU HAVE PROBABLY heard some of the following arguments that were born during the sexual revolution of the 1960's:.

+ "What difference does a little piece of paper like a marriage license make? When you're in love, isn't that all that matters?"

+ "Since we are committed to each other and we know we're going to get married anyway, it's okay."

A $1 bill and a $100 bill, in reality, are nothing more than two little pieces of paper. However, their value lies in the promises behind them.

What is the value of what used to be called holy matrimony? Unfortunately, postmodern Christians, taking their cues from the rhythms of the world, seem to need more socio-scientific rationale than just the Bible in order to know how to live out their sexuality.

I often wonder what the world would look like without the endless barrage of supermodel images on billboards and in magazines, shock radio, silicone implants, on-again-off-again

Hollywood relationships, or suggestive rap lyrics that tell us sex is the absolutely most important aspect of all human existence on the earth.

It's ironic that the same people who believe that premarital sexual activity is really no big deal will move heaven and earth to preserve the secret contents of a Christmas package, not to be opened until December 25th! Is the preservation of our sexuality less valuable than a Christmas present?

In America, we have a thing called statutory rape. It's where a twenty-one-year old (or older) adult, for example, gets locked away for taking "indecent liberties" with a fifteen-year-old. Yet no one gets arrested when the same fifteen-year-old fumbles around in the back seat of a parked car with a sixteen-year-old, as they test drive the new condoms they received at a government-initiated "safe sex" rally.

If you have not already noticed, marriage hardly matters anymore. The cultural push for the legal recognition of same-sex unions, for example, has already been endorsed by governments in Europe and New Zealand, to name a few.

But maybe, on the other hand, you are part of the remnant who have no intentions of going all the way before the wedding day. Nevertheless, you don't foresee any danger in spending time alone, away from other people, tempting one another with lots of touching and kissing while your favorite love song plays on the radio in the background. It is not my purpose to judge anyone, but I submit to you that if this is your standard, you are playing with fire.

Consider this. Your wedding day is simultaneously the finish line of one race and the starting line of another. The goal is to win both races! Victory in the first race is about you and your future spouse helping one another preserve more than just each other's sexual purity. But more so, it is meant to preserve that unique, new thing that has never existed since the beginning of time your sexual oneness. Do you remember the third entity from chapter 5? It is the heart and soul of your marriage. It is about what you create together when you become one. Jesus put it this way, quoting the Old Testament: "For this reason, a man shall leave his father and mother, and be joined to his wife. And they, two, shall become one flesh" (Matt. 19:5).

So, technically, what is the difference between two college kids "hooking up" in a Miami hotel room on spring break and the first honeymoon night of a newlywed, Bible-believing couple? *Mechanically*, there is probably not much difference. Emotionally, spiritually, and legacy-wise, it is the difference between night and day! The spring break scenario is all about "What I *get* out of the experience." The Christian marriage bed should be about how much of a blessing we can be to each other. Paul says we should consider the interest of others before our own interest. If two people are doing that for each other, both should be blessed in the end.

Joseph and Mary are probably the best biblical examples of engagement. They apparently had no intimate relations prior to marriage. They were both so committed to preserving the awakening of their sexual oneness until their marriage was official that it took an angel of the Lord to intervene and encourage Joseph to actually follow through with their plans to marry. He had to be convinced that Mary's pregnancy was both miraculous and God's doing.

Why is experiencing each other sexually for the first time at the right time (in marriage) so valuable? Other than the fact that the Scriptures command it, the kind of intimacy and trust that can be formed at that instant will provide a quality, firm foundation upon which to build your entire marriage! It is the perfect opportunity to establish what I call a "holy first."

The Bible is full of examples of the importance of firsts, such as first-born children and first-fruits offerings. The Book of

Acts notes the town in which Christ followers were "first called Christians" (Acts 11:26).

One of the things life teaches us is that we have only one chance to make a first impression. That is one of the reasons we advise engaged couples to plan to direct more resources toward their honeymoon days than they do the wedding day. Your first days of marriage together provide two unique opportunities:

- They set the tone for how you will function as a couple for your entire married lives.

- They become a reference point, positive or negative, for your marriage. If those early days are full of excitement, discovery, and intimacy, then you have established a track record that says, "It is possible for us to have a beautiful marriage together."

Have you noticed how, at least in Western society, so little thought is given to the future? The world says, "Forget about tomorrow. It's all about right now! Have your fun today. It's old-fashioned to discipline yourself to wait for anything. Why wait?" This kind of logic can be compounded when we look around and can hardly see any visible consequences to instant gratification.

Maybe we could learn something from Wall Street. There is an aspect of high finance and investing called futures. People smarter than I am have figured out a way to make financial decisions based on what they estimate the value of a particular thing will be at some point in the future. There is that word *value* again. Isn't marriage more valuable than money?

So, how do two engaged Christians, who see the value of getting it right, safeguard their future sexual oneness? Here are some tips.

God designed human sexual response to be relatively seamless.

It does not take a PhD in sexology to know that the standard progression toward sexual intimacy involves a certain amount of touching that somehow leads to kissing, then more intense touching. The lines between these stages are very blurry. After a while, the train is barreling downhill toward intercourse. All the response "equipment" is designed to follow a natural progression toward a glorious end. Pass a certain point, and euphoria takes over and begins to lead all activity rather than logic, Scripture memory verses, or even yellow wristbands that read "What Would Jesus Do?" If you are serious about preserving that holy first, where in this process should you draw the line? Does the Bible give any specific guidance? Perhaps a good initial Bible study would be the interaction between couples in the Scriptures who were also in some kind of premarital state: Isaac and Rebecca, Boaz and Ruth, David and Bathsheba, Esther and King Xerxes. I don't find many positive examples of these couples spending time alone together prior to marriage.

Agree together to swim against the popular stream.

Because you have graduated to a new level of commitment to one another, the natural tendency is to want to spend time alone together and away from other people. If you are not from a culture where parents and others are obliged to make certain that your engagement season is not compromised, then invite godly couples into your engagement, asking them to help you safeguard this time. You may have to go out of your way to establish new habits of spending little or no time alone together. You also might want to ask your accountability watchmen to help you establish specific boundaries in terms of your physical interaction together. If you want to talk privately, do so at a public kind of place where other people are around.

Don't set your wedding date more than six months or so away from your official engagement announcement.

No rocket science here. There are enough hurdles to clear during your engagement. What sense does it make to cause time to work against you in the race toward the first finish line?

Paul gives an excellent rule of thumb.

In 1 Timothy 5:1–2, Paul tells us, "Treat younger men as brothers, older women as mothers, and younger women as sisters, with absolute purity." In other words, gentlemen, don't do anything with your fiancé that you would not do with your sister. I realize that there are not many Hollywood movies that portray this kind of behavior, but this is simply what the Bible says.

What if you have already blown it in some way? Suppose your pre-Christian lifestyle was completely out of control? Suppose even your Christian lifestyle has been full of compromise and promiscuity. Is redemption and restoration possible? According to Romans 8, Yes it is. The apostle Paul deemed himself the chief of sinners. First John 1:9 declares that "If we confess our sins, He is faithful and just and will forgive us our sins and purify us from all unrighteousness." How awesome is that?

Nevertheless, like any other sin, there may be some irreversible consequences to actions that we have engaged in. Unintended pregnancies, sexually transmitted diseases, and even HIV/AIDS infection can be some of the lingering results of following the world's lead.

SEXUALLY TRANSMITTED DISEASE

If you forget most of what this book has presented, remember this! If you have been sexually active at all prior to marriage, you need to be clinically tested well before the wedding day—before you become sexually active in your marriage. Several sexually transmitted diseases are not 100 percent protected by using condoms.

+ FACT: One out of four females in the U.S. between the age of fifteen and nineteen have an STD.

+ FACT: By age twenty-five, half of all sexually active adults get an STD.

+ FACT: Many carriers of some STDs experience no noticeable signs of infection. If left untreated, some of these STDs can lead to infertility, cancer, and even death.

+ FACT: Some STDs spread through any kind of skin-to-skin contact, including kissing and oral sex.

+ FACT: Bacterial STD infections can be cleared up with treatment. Viral STD infections remain with the infected person for life (no cure).[1]

How unfair and careless would it be to pass on a viral infection to your spouse because of ignorance? If you have been sexually active outside of marriage, *get tested!*

If, however, you have managed to pass through the gauntlet of sexual temptation with your sexual purity intact, keep it that way. I have never heard a married person express regret for having maintained their sexual purity all the way to their wedding day. I have, however, witnessed the tears and guilt of those who wish they had.

The following list of discussion topics is designed to be used in a premarital "coaching" situation. The engaged couple is to answer these questions separate from each other—*not together.* The engaged couple should not discuss their answers at all prior to doing so together with their coaching "mentor" couple. (Allow approximately one week to complete the answers.) The "mentor couple" should be a couple whose own marriage is godly and who have the experience of having raised children themselves. (The character and reputation of their teen-to-adult kids can serve as a true test of their ability to guide the couple with real authority.) Often, Christians do their premarital counseling sessions with a pastor or one person. I believe it's important for there to be both a man and a woman (who are married to each other) involved in their marriage prep coaching.

The couple should submit their answers to a godly married couple who can guide the engaged couple's discussion of each question and answer them, one by one. (There will most often need to be several scheduled sessions together in order to get through the entire document).

1. Children

+ Are we going to have children? (Yes, No, Maybe)
+ I want to start having children:
    a. immediately
    b. _____ year(s) after we marry
    c. whenever God gives them
    d. never

+ My philosophy on the matter of birth control is (_____).
+ I want to have (#)_____ children
+ I want our children to be educated in the following way (choose one):
    a. homeschool
    b. public school
    c. private school

d. some other way

* I think children should be disciplined in the following way: _____

2. Sex

* I am expecting us to engage in sexual activity (mark as many as apply to your expectation—there can be more than one):
    a. every day
    b. several times a day
    c. once a week (on average)
    d. more than once a week
    e. once a month
    f. more than once a month
    g. whenever I want to, whether my marriage partner wants to or not
    h. whenever my marriage partner wants to, whether I want to or not
    i. never

* (Yes or No) In my opinion, sex is a "need" (explain your answer)

* During the woman's menstruation period, I expect:
    a. that we will abstain from sexual activity during those times
    b. that we will continue having sex during those times

* While the woman is pregnant, I expect:
    a. that we will abstain from sexual activity during those times
    b. that we will continue having sex during those

times (It is medically recommended that a woman not engage in any sexual intercourse for at least six weeks after childbirth.)

+ It is my current understanding that my fiancé/ fiancée (select one only):

    a. has never been sexually active before

    b. has been sexually active before

    c. I don't really know

+ Regarding my fiancé/fiancée's previous sexual experience:

    a. I want to know everything about it

    b. I don't want to know anything about it

    c. I think we should discuss it, but not necessarily in detail

+ If I personally feel that we are having problems sexually in our marriage, I think we should (choose as many options as you feel apply to your opinion):

    a. agree ahead of time to only seek advice and input together

    b. agree ahead of time to only seek advice and input individually, apart from each other

    c. only pray about it and trust God to make the problem go away

    d. discuss the problem together to see if we can solve it ourselves; if that doesn't work, then seek outside advice

3. Money (income earning, future, day-to-day, insurance, debt)

(Indicate Yes or No to each statement. Explain your choice when necessary.)

- I think we should make all financial decisions together
- All of our financial accounts should be joint
- I think we should each have separate accounts that we individually control
- I am the best one to be in charge of our money
- I think we must always tithe on our income
- It's okay to borrow money
- It is okay for each of us to bring debt into our marriage
- I expect that we will only rent homes for our entire marriage
- I expect that we will own our home(s)
- We should always save money
- We should agree to seek help if we find ourselves in financial problems
- We will be able to solve our financial problems by ourselves without any help
- I expect my spouse to talk to me before making any major purchase

4. In-laws/extended family (holidays, emergency obligations, etc.)

- I expect my spouse's family to (choose as many as reflect your expectation):

    a. be very involved in our lives together

    b. visit often

    c. leave us alone

    d. be a bit of a problem

    e. help us when we need it

    f. live with us for indefinite periods of time

    g. live with us temporarily in times of emergency

    h. be free to borrow money from us if they need to

    i. help us if we need help

+ I expect my family to (choose as many as reflect your expectation):

    a. be very involved in our lives together

    b. visit often

    c. leave us alone

    d. be a bit of a problem

    e. help us when we need it

    f. live with us for indefinite periods of time

    g. live with us temporarily in times of emergency

    h. be free to borrow money from us if they need to

    i. help us if we need help

5. Friends

+ I expect my spouse's friends to (choose as many as reflect your expectation):

    a. be very involved in our lives together

    b. visit often

    c. leave us alone

    d. be a bit of a problem

    e. help us when we need it

    f. live with us for indefinite periods of time

    g. live with us temporarily in times of emergency

    h. be free to borrow money from us if they need to

    i. help us if we need help

    j. spend time with my spouse apart from me
       (occasionally; daily; never)

- I expect my friends to (choose as many as reflect your expectation):

    a. be very involved in our lives together
    b. visit often
    c. leave us alone
    d. be a bit of a problem
    e. help us when we need it
    f. live with us for indefinite periods of time
    g. live with us temporarily in times of emergency
    h. be free to borrow money from us if they need to
    i. help us if we need help
    j. spend time with me apart from my spouse
       (occasionally; daily; never)

6. Politics (voting, etc.)

- I expect that we will be:

    a. very involved with politics
    b. not involved with politics at all
    c. somewhat involved with politics

7. Religion/faith

- Describe, in detail, your expectations regarding:

    a. church attendance and membership
    b. family worship
    c. Bible reading together
    d. individual devotions and personal worship
    e. denominational alliances
    f. charitable giving

8. Wedding

+ Be prepared to discuss as many of the following topics that are important to you:
    a. I want our wedding to be very small and private (just the two of us and an official pastor, etc.)
    b. I want our wedding to only have close family and friends attending
    c. I want our wedding to be very big and as grand as financially possible
    d. _____ is/am/are financially responsible to pay for our wedding
    e. Our wedding date will be approximately _____ from now.

+ My expectations regarding a honeymoon are:
    a. No time or money for a honeymoon
    b. I want to stay close to home
    c. I want to go someplace far away
    d. I want to go away for a short time (how short?)
    e. I want to go away for a long time (how long?)
    f. I want to spend lots of time sightseeing and going on adventures that are new to both of us
    g. I want to spend most of our time resting and taking life slowly

9. Domestic responsibilities (meal prep, cleaning, repairs, decoration/design)

+ I think _____ should do all the cooking and meal preparation.
+ I think _____ should do all the laundry and house cleaning.

- I think _____ should do any home repairs and auto maintenance.

- The decorating and interior design of our home should mostly be done by _____.

- When the baby cries in the middle of the night and needs feeding, I expect _____ to get up and take care of that.

- When the baby's diaper needs to be changed I expect _____ to take care of that (most/all) of the time.

- (Yes or No) I want us to eat most of our meals together at a table where we share conversation together without television and/or any other kinds of distractions like Internet, iPod, or telephone conversations with others during the meal time.

- (Choose the one that most fits your expectation) I expect us to eat out (at restaurants, etc.):
  a. never
  b. most of the time
  c. sometimes

10. Recreation and leisure time
(Choose any statements that describe your feeling)

- I hate exercise and physical activity

- I want us to do all our fun and play together

- I am open to my spouse going off for recreational activity without me

- I hate to be alone

- Spending time by myself occasionally is refreshing to me

- I expect my spouse and me to do everything together
- I think wearing matching clothes proves that we really love each other.
- We sometimes will need to go on long trips together, just for fun.
- My idea of family fun together is

  _____.

11. Divorce

(In detail, describe your philosophy on this. Is it an option, or do you feel that it should never be an option, no matter what?)

- Describe in writing how far you are willing to go to work out your differences in order to avoid divorce.
- If our relationship comes to a point where we need to live separately for a while, I:
  a. will refuse to do that
  b. am willing to do that only if it will help my partner have time to think about ways we can improve our relationship
  c. am willing to do that for (#)_____ (days/ weeks/months/years) maximum, before I think we should really get back together again.

- The only thing that would make me desire divorce is _____. (explain)

12. Crisis counseling

- If our marriage is in trouble, I am willing to _____. (write detail)

+ If my spouse thinks we need counseling but I don't think we need it (chose one only):
  a. I am willing to go to counseling anyway.
  b. I refuse to talk to anyone else about our marriage. It's none of their business.

13. Unexpected illness/accident/injury (living will)

+ If for some reason I am too sick to make my own decisions (coma, life support, etc.), this is what I want my spouse to do:

+ If my spouse becomes sick for an indefinite length of time, I commit to caring for them myself (for how long?)

Although this is *not a legally binding contract*, my signature and date below means that my spouse or I may bring this document out at any time to *gently remind* one another of what our understanding and expectations were, prior to marriage.

Write your thoughts on any other topic that you feel is important to discuss before marriage:

(Your Name/Signature) _____

(Date) _____

(Fiancé/Fiancée's Signature) _____

(Date) _____

(Male Coaches' Signature) _____

(Date) _____

(Female Coaches' Signature) _____

(Date) _____

This process is best done with a husband-and-wife team doing the coaching, not just one gender or the other. There may be sessions you will want to do man-to-man, woman-to-woman only.

Notes

CHAPTER 1—WHY MARRIAGE?

1. Fabiola Hernandez, "Countries Where Same-Sex Marriage Is Legal," *Associated Content*, May 21, 2009, accessed April 5, 2011, http://www.associatedcontent.com/article/1763482/countries_where_samesex_marriage_is_pg2.html?cat=7.

2. Jessica Garrison and Dan Morain, "Same-sex Marriage Total at 11,000: California Reaches the Number in Three Months, Surpassing Massachusetts over Four Years, Study Finds," *LA Times*, October 7, 2008, accessed March 16, 2011, http://articles.latimes.com/2008/oct/07/local/me-gaymarriage7.

3. *Cohabitation, Marriage, and Child Wellbeing: A Cross-National Perspective*, by The National Marriage Project, Rutgers University (2008).

CHAPTER 12—NOW THAT YOU'RE ENGAGED, WHY WAIT FOR THE WEDDING NIGHT?

1. Facts in list derived from websites: www.webmd.com and www.cdc.gov, (accessed March, 1, 2011).

About the Author

KENNY JACKSON WAS born and raised in the United States, near Washington D.C. He became a follower of Jesus Christ at the age of seventeen after observing how faith in Jesus completely transformed his father, who was radically set free from an addiction to gambling. At age nineteen, Kenny joined Youth With A Mission, eventually making YWAM Hong Kong his home mission base from 1983 to 1992. During those years of ministry in and around Hong Kong, Kenny married fellow YWAM'er, Maria, who is from Seoul, South Korea. Kenny and Maria's cross-cultural marriage of twenty-four years has ministered to thousands as they have traveled to more than thirty countries together. Eventually, Kenny's gifts and calling to the arts developed into a passion for film and television production. After earning a Master's degree at Regent University's School of Cinema, Television, and Theatre Arts, Kenny began working professionally, producing and directing evangelistic television movies for The Christian Broadcasting Network (CBN).

Kenny and Maria have three children and live in Kailua-Kona, Hawaii.

Contact the Author

kingdomsexuality@aol.com

Published in association with
Patti M. Hummel, President/Agent
The Benchmark Group
Nashville, TN
benchmarkgroup1@aol.com